The Professional Schools

The Professional Schools

WILLIAM J. *oseph* MCGLOTHLIN

Vice-President
University of Louisville

The Center for Applied Research in Education, Inc.
New York

LIBRARY OF CONGRESS
CATALOG CARD NO.: 64-22131

PRINTED IN THE UNITED STATES OF AMERICA

Foreword

It is characteristic of modern society that it provides, encourages, and even demands more and more formal preparation for more and more occupations. This is partly because the technical skills required have become more numerous and more complex. It is partly because the tasks to be performed require the command of more analytical power. It is partly, no doubt, because of the prestige that education has come to possess and has proved able to bestow on its recipients.

Whenever the point is reached at which the amount of time allowed for preparation for an occupation equals or exceeds that required for study for a bachelor's degree, several things tend to happen. The question arises as to whether the program of instruction ought not to be taken over by the university and its successful completion recognized by the award of a degree. And—especially if that question is answered in the affirmative—the occupation begins to lay claim to the status of a profession.

The university in the United States has been particularly willing to establish divisions designed to prepare for an ever increasing variety of lines of work. These are customarily referred to in the aggregate as "the professional schools," being thus distinguished from the college of arts and sciences and its succeeding graduate program. The considerable majority of students in a large American university will be enrolled in such schools.

It is with education for the professions as provided by the university that this book is concerned. It examines systematically the major questions which deans and members of the faculties of professional schools need continually to consider and reconsider. It explains the issues and takes positions on them. And—a particular merit—it constantly relates its parts to a whole, to a theory of what the aims of professional education should be.

The author writes as an experienced university administrator who

v

has long pondered his subject. What he writes can be read with interest and profit by all to whom education for the professions is a concern, whether within or without the university.

KARL W. BIGELOW
Teachers College,
Columbia University

The Professional Schools

William J. McGlothlin

Mr. McGlothlin's book treats comprehensively the programs for preparing practitioners in the recognized professions in the United States. The treatment is comparative, showing differences as well as likenesses in the curriculums for some sixteen professions, such as medicine, engineering, social work, teaching, and nursing. Particularly interesting is the discussion of the sometimes conflicting goals of providing a sufficient quantity of professional service and of maintaining a high quality of practice in the profession.

The book stresses the historical background of preparation for the professions, showing how the present program evolved from the older apprenticeship system. The author points out that present practices and procedures are largely a product of the Twentieth Century, having been stimulated by the pioneer work of Abraham Flexner in medical education. The book presents relatively complete descriptions of present situations, and makes some cautious forecasts about future developments. The author does not hesitate to criticize present conditions that, on the basis of his evidence, seem to him to be in need of correction. A distinctive feature of the book is the statement of principles appearing as a summary at the end of each chapter.

The Professional Schools is one of three books in the Library of Education that deal with broad aspects of the instructional programs of American Colleges and Universities. Dr. Paul Dressel's book, *The Undergraduate Curriculum in Higher Education,* treats the four-year sequence immediately following high school graduation. The series also has another volume on Graduate Education.

JOHN DALE RUSSELL
Content Editor

Contents

CHAPTER I

Origin and Characteristics of Professions

The professions are outgrowths of society's needs or desires for special services. Probably the first of the professions was that of the medicine man, who served his society by acting as mediary between man and the forces of nature which man could neither understand nor escape. His skilled incantations were passed from father to son through generation after generation. The patient obtained comfort, if not health, through the power of his professional care.

The professional soldier also appeared early in history. Many of the Greek legends tell the exploits of the professional soldier, who plied his trade far from home and brought glory back with him. As the medicine man protected his society from disease and death, so the soldier protected his society from the ravages of hostile groups. He, too, learned his professional skills by observation and experience, since little theory of war developed in written form. The Old Testament, however, describes the selection of an elite army long before the entrance examinations for West Point or Annapolis were considered. As the story goes, Gideon tested his soldiers by letting them drink from a stream. He chose the few who remained alert, scooping up water with their hands without moving their eyes from the direction of the enemy. The others, who knelt on the bank to drink directly from the stream, he left behind.[1]

The military profession is directly descended from the soldier of yesterday, even though the complexities of war have increased enormously since the time of Gideon. But the medicine man's descent is divided into two paths—one leading to the temple and the other to the apothecary. The path that led to the temple turned the medicine man into the priest, a position defined by special garb and ascetic life. He lived apart in the monasteries and served as mediator between the occult powers and man much as his ancestor had done. At times, through miraculous events, he reappeared as a medicine

---

[1] *Judges.* Chapter 7, verses 4–8.

1

man. The other path led the medicine man to the role of a physician, a role which began to eschew the occult and employ observation and drugs to assist the body to conquer its maladies. As he turned from magic to medicine, he differentiated himself from the priest. He served to restore and maintain health, while the priest presided at all major functions of existence, from birth to death. Two professions grew from one, since, as society's needs increased, one group could not supply both services.

Society in its early simplicity could subsist with few special services and therefore few professional groups. As its complexity increased, the number of professions grew. Biblical literature refers to the soldier, the scholar, the lawyer, the priest, the tax collector, and many others. By the Middle Ages, Chaucer could describe in his *Canterbury Tales* the Man of Law, the Doctor, and the Clerk. Some of his other pilgrims are also members of professions—particularly the clergy, and business is represented by the Merchant. During the Middle Ages, the great universities of Europe were established to transfer the knowledge and lore of the professions from practitioners and scholars to students who wished to qualify for a particular profession. Theology, medicine, and law had become the dominant professions, and the universities undertook to educate men to enter them.[2]

Professions arose, then, when a group of men was recognized as having unusual abilities to assuage the hurts and calm the fears of others by mediating among them and between them and the powers of the universe. Those powers were ever-present; they had to be propitiated or disaster would befall. Their strength was clearly evident in the eruptions of thunderstorms and volcanoes and in the sudden enfeebling of vigorous men. The powers were most fearful when they struck dead those who but a moment before laughed and loved. No lay person could command these powers; they were beyond ordinary control. Only those with special preparation and magic gifts could hope to deal with them. Only the medicine man could be of help.

Beginning, therefore, with the medicine man, the professional man has been a person of unusual gifts. His primary characteristic is special competence, his ability to act in certain useful ways which

[2] Hastings Rashdall, *The Universities of Europe in the Middle Ages* (Oxford: Clarendon Press, 1895).

he has achieved by extraordinary dispensation or effort. His is not the competence of ordinary men. His competence is special.

Because he has special competence, society allows the professional man to have a monopoly in his service. Only he and those with his skills and knowledge are permitted to practice. The monopoly is intended to prevent quacks and quackery and prohibit the unlearned from endangering the client and casting doubt upon the whole profession by shoddy performance of its tasks. Also, the monopoly protects men of high ability from unwarranted encroachment once they become worthy of admission into the profession. Thus, a physician will spend ten to twelve years acquiring his professional competence because he knows that only equally educated men are allowed the privileges of the profession. Without this protection he can hardly function, for he would be placed in competition with others whose skills are less and whose training easier. He would not be willing to defer his entrance into the profession in order to conclude his training if he were not later protected against untrained competitors.

Other groups in modern society have special competencies but are not considered professions. More detailed descriptions are needed to distinguish professions from other occupations. One of the earliest attempts, dating from 1915, comes from Dr. Abraham Flexner, who by that time had begun to revolutionize medical education in the United States. Dr. Flexner distinguished professions from occupations by applying a set of six criteria. In his view, a profession is *intellectual,* and carries with it great personal responsibility for the proper exercise of choice and judgment. It is *learned,* for it is based on a substantial body of knowledge, developed over a long period of years and transmissible to students who wish to enter the profession. Incidentally, this means that training for a profession is customarily long and arduous. In the medieval university, the curriculum in law required ten years' time to complete. A profession is *practical,* since its knowledge can be applied to real-life situations in the here and now. In other words, it can help solve human problems. A profession also has *techniques,* or skills, which can be taught, and which serve as the mechanisms by which knowledge can be applied to the solution of problems. It is *organized* into associations or groups of practitioners for various professional purposes, including those of guiding the education of students and regulating entrance into the profession. And last, but extremely important, a profession is guided by *altruism,* by concern for the patients or clients who come to it for help. Its purpose is to benefit mankind.[3]

One characteristic should be added to Flexner's formulation. A profession *deals with matters of great urgency and significance.* Baby sitters, barbers, beauticians, or bartenders can never be considered as members of professions since their ministrations, although frequently desired and sometimes pleasant, are hardly matters of utmost importance. To be sure, the world would look different if men grew beards and chopped their hair off at their shoulders, but it would not be an essential change. These occupations do not deal with matters of sufficient moment, as do the professions of medicine and nursing, for example. Medicine and nursing preside over birth and death and much in between. Other professions deal with equally significant affairs. Law is concerned with the administration of justice and the resolution of conflict without violence; the ministry helps mankind aspire to its highest values; architecture encloses space for human use.[4] The last characteristic, then, is that professions deal with significant problems.

These seven characteristics distinguish the professions from other occupations. Professions are intellectual, learned, and practical. They have techniques that can be taught; their members are organized into associations; they are guided by altruism, and they deal with matters of great human urgency. These characteristics allow modern society to legalize monopoly through the licensing of professional people much as the earlier societies permitted only a sharply restricted number of medicine men. A profession is master of a difficult and extensive body of knowledge, over which it has exclusive control. No one can execute the tasks assigned to the profession without this knowledge and no one can acquire the knowledge without the profession's approval. Only members of a profession can perform its tasks and these tasks are so crucially important that society would suffer painfully if they were not executed, or if they were executed poorly.

---

[3] Adapted from Abraham Flexner, "Is Social Work a Profession?" *Proceedings of the National Conference of Charities and Correction* (Chicago: The Hildmann Printing Co., 1915), pp. 576–590.

[4] Adapted from William J. McGlothlin, "The Place of Nursing Among the Professions," *Nursing Outlook,* Vol. 9 (April, 1961).

Under this monopoly, the profession controls the body of knowledge on which its practice rests, and controls the number and kind of persons who are allowed to study. It controls admission to the profession through accrediting schools and directing licensing of individuals by the state, since the licensing boards are usually dominated by members of the professions. Through all these means, the profession controls matters which concern it with virtually no interference from lay persons. Such a monopoly can be justified by the argument that no lay person has the knowledge on which the profession rests, and therefore no lay person can judge what should be done.

Monopoly is necessary for the professions, but it is supportable only because of their altruism. Society allows a profession to be a monopoly because it is convinced that the profession is dedicated to an ethical, or altruistic, ideal in serving society. Society is reassured because the altruism of the profession is expressed through a code whose purpose, among other ends, is to protect the public from exploitation. If a profession does not enforce its code, its monopoly is endangered. The profession's ethics, its code, is at the very heart of its professional practice. Without it a profession could turn from benefiting society into self-seeking—from altruism into exploitation. In so doing it would number its days. A society will find other ways of obtaining services if a profession ignores the fact that its privileges are awarded for so long as it aids and serves but does not exploit its clientele.

CHAPTER II

The Purpose of Professions

The professions have characteristics which arise from the purposes they are expected to serve. These purposes are fairly easy to define.

Satisfying Needs

The first purpose of a profession is to supply the society with services, skills, or facilities which satisfy important needs or desires of the members of that society. Initially, a profession focuses on the needs of individuals. A physician is usually called to deal with developed illness; a lawyer to deal with imminent conflicts. The professional relationship includes the practitioner and the client. It has little to do with anyone else. Therefore, the professional person customarily receives a fee. He sets the size of his fee and may withhold his services if he wishes. The fee also is used to evaluate the effectiveness of his services, since presumably he will attract fees from patients or clients only if he is skilled and diligent. Even the teacher, who is now paid a salary by a school system or a private school, was originally either a tutor working with the son of his patron or an itinerant school master, finding employment where he could after virtually organizing the group of pupils himself.

These services, like those of the architect, the minister, or the nurse, arose to satisfy needs of individuals. Nursing, for example, was born out of the urgencies of war. Later, the nurse expanded her care to the populace at large. At first she, too, worked largely with individuals in their homes, but when she transferred her relationship to the hospital, she was able to serve many more patients than the sharply limited numbers she could reach in homes. By grouping patients and clients into institutions, other professions have also extended their social usefulness. Thus physicians and a number of other professions came to use the hospital for their practice, and teachers organized schools to which the pupils came. In this way, professions broadened their attention from individuals to groups. To be sure, the individual might receive less immediate and separate attention in the institutions, but he could count on more varied services.

Even more significantly, however, the professions expended great effort to reduce problems through modifying causes rather than limiting themselves to treating effects. Henrik Ibsen, in 1882, wrote *An Enemy of the People* to portray the fate of a physician who sacrificed himself to save his town from a polluted water supply. Long before Ibsen, the Romans brought pure water through miles of stone viaducts into Rome, recognizing the relationship of pure water with health. Medicine has instituted and supported prevention of disease through public health programs; social work has supplemented individual casework with social legislation that prevents the rise of need; dentistry has urged cities to fluoridate their water supplies to reduce dental decay; lawyers through legislation have attempted to reduce the areas in which litigation is inevitable; architects have become city planners to help make pleasant living possible for a community as a whole; and government, with the backing of the professions concerned, has established and enforced pure food and drug laws. The social usefulness of the professions, then, has been extended through concentrating clients in hospital, school, and church and through modifying the environment in such ways that problems are reduced or prevented.

A profession remains vital by increasing the social usefulness of its activities. A physician who finds the connection between polluted water and typhoid fever, and develops a serum to protect large numbers of persons from the disease, has extended the significance of medicine beyond the contribution which treating individual cases can ever make. Medicine's advances in this direction have been so rapid that many contagious diseases which once plagued the United States have almost disappeared. The work of Salk and Sabin on polio vaccines illustrates this great advance.

Many professions cannot eliminate a need for their services since they are intended to bring positive benefits rather than to eradicate evils such as illness. But even they can find ways to extend and supplement their services by other efforts. Teachers will always be needed because the child will always seek to learn his way through the complex world around him. But the interest of the teacher in educating youth through schools can be extended to developing libraries where one can learn for oneself, to the use of television for educational programs, to the distribution of books cheaply through the publishing revolution of paper backs, and so on. A profession cannot be fully satisfied with a one-to-one relationship among its practitioners and beneficiaries. The costs are too great and the benefits too narrow. Each profession must search for ways to expand its benefits, both through removing the causes of evil and through extending the influence of good.

Advancing Knowledge

These objectives inevitably lead the professions to their second purpose—to advance knowledge within the fields. Even in the one-to-one relationship, a profession struggles to better its service, guided as it is by the purpose of social usefulness. No profession is ever satisfied that it has given as much as it can. It constantly strives for new and more effective methods. To find them, it must advance the knowledge in its field through systematic observation and experimentation—in other words, through research.

The medicine man had little theory or skill with which to conduct a research program. He could, and probably did, observe those incantations which appeared to have the greatest success, and he undoubtedly passed these observations to his successors. Through this means he built a body of magic lore that substituted for knowledge. The medicine man, however, could not conduct research on continuing problems since he was unable to develop a theory which satisfactorily explained known facts or pointed to areas which needed further exploration. Modern medicine itself had to await the development of satisfactory theory. So long as medicine believed that the explanation of disease lay in the balance among the four humours—blood, phlegm, yellow bile, and black bile—it could hardly isolate the causes of the ailments it observed. Once the germ theory of disease was constructed the profession was able to discover means of reducing the incidence of the contagious diseases and of offsetting their destructiveness to the human system.

Following the lead of medicine, most professions have adopted the purpose of advancing knowledge. Engineering considers itself one of the physical sciences. It has that right because it contributes directly to knowledge in the physical sciences, particularly in physics and chemistry. Engineering is no longer limited by manuals of procedure. It adds knowledge which it shares with other physical sciences.

Nursing has recognized its obligation to advance knowledge by assessing its members in support of research projects. Many of the annual drives for the voluntary health agencies emphasize that the funds will be spent not on service but on research. The professions encourage this policy, since they hope to advance the effectiveness of their practices through research. Practitioners who sneer at the research man are decreasing in number. They can hardly continue to sneer when their practice depends upon such results of research as penicillin, radioactive cobalt, Skinner's pigeons at Harvard, or the splitting of atoms. The distance from laboratory to practice has become shorter than ever before, and the professions incorporate more and more research activity in their purpose of advancing knowledge.

Protecting Members and Practice

Finally, a profession has the purpose of protecting its members and making it possible for them to practice effectively. Its protection must take a number of forms, for the profession may suffer from internal as well as external dangers. Internally, the profession must protect members against the incompetent or dishonest member, whose actions will damage trust in the profession. For example, a dishonest lawyer chips away at the faith which clients must maintain in their attorneys. Without trust, a client may withhold vital evidence, and thereby prevent the attorney from representing him effectively. For the sake of all its members, the legal profession must do its best to prevent dishonest practice.

The profession also protects members against individuals and groups which try to encroach on the area of the profession and to practice without competence to do so.[1] In addition, the profession opposes efforts to establish conditions which would make practice

---

[1] Suppression of quacks has long concerned the professions. In England in 1423, the Guild of Physicians and Surgeons petitioned the King to "suppress quacks and empiriks and the knavish men and women who doe presume to practice some sort of Physick." Quoted in W.S.C. Copeman, *Doctors and Disease in Tudor Times* (London: Dawson's of Pall Mall, 1960), p. 31.

difficult or impossible. The profession controls admission to prevent incompetent persons from entering the profession and to avoid such an oversupply of practitioners that none could obtain sufficient income to live comfortably. Lawyers oppose any effort to remove their right of privileged communication, since their effectiveness as advocates depends on their being able to learn all the facts, even those which are most damaging to their clients. Teachers oppose efforts to limit their right to freedom of study and teaching. Professions sometimes object to the idea of lay control because they fear that someone who cannot understand the requirements of practice will be unable to act in their best interests. A profession bitterly fights against encroachment by other groups. Each profession defines an area of practice in which it has a monopoly and it fights hard to preserve that unique status. Without that status, its usefulness declines.

Professional associations aid practitioners to obtain legal sanction for their monopoly. Once a profession is awarded legal status and is given the exclusive right to practice in the field of its competence, it can destroy the practice of frauds by submitting them to trial and punishment by the courts. It licenses or certifies appropriately trained members of the profession and excludes the rest. It has an obligation to police its own ranks, to make certain that those who wear the name and display the license are in fact ethical and competent practitioners. From this obligation stem efforts to enforce the code of ethics of the profession even by expelling members who flagrantly violate provisions of its code. A physician can "lose his license." A lawyer can be disbarred. The number of cases in any one year is small, but the fact that they occur is witness to the professions' effort to protect their members even from erring colleagues.

Most of this effort lies in enforcing the code of ethics. Little is done with exposing incompetence. Medicine has struggled for years with the problem. Through licensing practitioners and accrediting schools, it tries to make sure that those who enter are qualified to practice. Hippocrates apparently observed the problem in his day. He said

> Medicine is of all Arts the most noble; but, owing to the ignorance of those who practice it, and of those who, inconsiderately, form a judgment of them, it is at present far behind the other arts. Their mistake appears to me to arise principally from this, that in

the cities there is no punishment connected with the practice of medicine . . . except disgrace, and that does not hurt those that are familiar with it.[2]

There is punishment now, largely administered by the profession itself, for unethical behavior, but not often for incompetence.

The present purposes of the professions are therefore (1) to unite competent people to do socially significant work of increasing usefulness, (2) to advance knowledge through research, and (3) to protect their members from unwarranted attack, unethical practice, encroachment, or quackery. The first and third of these are familiar purposes. The second—research—is more recent, and its impact on the educational programs for the professions has not yet reached its full effect. It may become equally influential in time. Certainly the public expects more effective professional practice in the future than it has received in the past. The public has become too sophisticated to allow the professions to avoid the effort of constant advance. Furthermore, government and private donors have contributed such huge sums to research in the professions that they have established the purpose of advancing knowledge so firmly that it can never again be ignored.

---

[2] Hippocrates, *The Law,* Vol. II, p. 784. Quoted in William B. Wartman, *Medical Teaching in Western Civilization* (Chicago: Yearbook Medical Publishers, 1961), p. 18.

CHAPTER III

The Aims of Professional Education

Development

The professions did not develop their present status overnight. Even the purposes for which the professions were organized changed substantially as society placed greater and greater dependence upon them. Earlier, as Hippocrates complained, all too many practiced the profession of medicine, and surely other professional fields also, with little competence and no feeling of disgrace when fraud was exposed. The need for learning the skills of practice became more and more evident, however, as knowledge accumulated. Serious professional students, like Galen in medicine, toured the world in search of teachers they wished to follow. Such teaching was unorganized and personal; it had more of the character of the craft apprenticeship than of the university. The word "school" referred to a group of scientists or practitioners rather than to an organized institution of learning. The form of instruction was that of practitioner and helper rather than that of teacher and class, since the student assisted in the work of the practitioner he admired and learned by emulation of the master.

As the numbers of students increased and demands for the professions grew, the preceptor-student organization of teaching became inadequate. It could not train all the students who wished to learn, and it was subsequently supplanted by the medieval university. These universities were basically professional schools— Salerno for medicine, Bologna for law, and Paris for theology.

In Bologna, for example, Socrates' inductive teaching method through question and discussion was lost in the need to teach large groups of students. The new procedure was to read to them from the books of civil and ecclesiastical law. Any originality appeared in the glosses, or interpretations, which the teacher wrote on the margins of his text. In the early days of these universities, books were largely in the possession of the teachers, and the students learned by writing down, almost verbatim, the readings which the teacher presented from the lectern. These discourses became known as lectures, and have remained the favorite form of teaching in universities. The medieval student had one advantage, however. If he did not like the instruction, he and his fellows could move the whole university, leaving the teachers behind. In fact, the word "university" is derived from the name of the student guild, *universitas,* rather than from any fancied conviction that the university was the repository of universal knowledge.

Professional schools of the middle ages grew up around the function of the church in several places, particularly in Paris, where the church needed theological schools to teach budding ecclesiastics the arguments which would convert the unbelievers. The purpose, again, was to educate competent practitioners.

In other places and in later times, the need of practitioners for assistance led to the professional school. This was a return, actually, to the earlier preceptorship with which education in medicine began. Schools of architecture apparently began when architects in France needed assistants to help them in their work. The fame of the French *Beaux Arts* School was so great that students came in large numbers, lured by the possibility of entering a lucrative and prestigious profession. Medical schools in Europe still accept large numbers of students but fail a very high percentage of them by the end of the first year. Where the skills of such students were once needed to help the practitioner, now their funds are required to support the university. For example, some European schools admit as many as three thousand medical students to the first year of study. Perhaps two hundred will graduate four years hence.

Out of the practitioner's workshop grew the proprietary school, which was operated by a group of practitioners who gave lectures and demonstrations for persons interested in entering the profession. The fees which supported the proprietary school were paid by students, and no one was tempted, therefore, to make the entrance standards very strict. The proprietary school attracted fame and money to its practitioners. It often did little to satisfy the educational needs of its students.

In the United States at the turn of the twentieth century, the proprietary school dominated professional education. Universities were not sure that the addition of professional schools would glorify their name. They had reason for scepticism. Much of the professional education of the day was so shoddy and narrow that no self-respecting university would have been willing to embrace it. The proprietary school in many of its manifestations exploited students for the gain of the faculty. Also, a university which incorporated a professional school inevitably incurred the antipathy of practitioners who saw the university as a threat to their proprietary schools. Not all members of the professions were satisfied with the state of affairs. In the United States, the Johns Hopkins University had been established as a graduate school and a medical school, and its influence was to do much toward remodeling medical education. Furthermore, in 1905, the American Medical Association established a means of accrediting medical schools. The movement to improve professional schools had therefore already started when Abraham Flexner published his deservedly famous report on *Medical Education in the United States and Canada* in 1910.[1] His invective, based on personal observation and analysis, caused the early collapse of many schools, and made it virtually impossible to operate a school on student fees alone. Dr. Flexner proposed two revolutionary steps—careful selection of students with at least two years of college work behind them, and expansion of work in the biological sciences, with adequate laboratory as well as classroom instruction. Both steps were expensive. Neither could be attempted by the practitioner alone. When biological scientists became part of the medical school faculty, when laboratories were built for teaching, when libraries were accumulated, and when students were selected on their competence to profit from instruction, the days of the proprietary school were numbered, and the numbers have diminished. Only in such relatively uncomplicated occupations as secretarial work or TV repair has it been possible for the proprietary school to continue.

As standards rose the old informal ways of learning a profession, such as "reading law" in an attorney's office or learning engineering "on the job," also disappeared. In their stead blossomed the professional school as part of the university. Even the public single-purpose professional schools, such as those in teacher education, law, medicine, and engineering, began to expand into complex institutions as they increased their attention to the sciences underlying

---

[1] Abraham Flexner, *Medical Education in the United States and Canada* (Boston: Updyke, Merrymount Press, 1910).

their fields. The professional school in the university became the usual pattern of professional education, except in a few fields like nursing where a noneducational institution—the hospital—has provided the bulk of the training. In nursing, however, several university programs supplement the hospital.

As these shifts occurred, the professional schools took on a new obligation that shortly was reflected in their aims. At first, their goal had been to aid the practitioner by providing him with a ready source of assistants. The proprietary school supplemented but did not take the place of many other ways of entering the professions. But as the professions moved into licensed occupations, rigidly excluding persons who had not been able to attain adequate levels of competence, the school accepted a commitment to supply adequate numbers of trained entrants. The school guaranteed the quality of the members of the profession. Its approval, defined by a degree or certificate, became a prerequisite of the licensing examination and a necessity on the practitioner's wall. Gradually, the professional school, in many fields, became the sole means of entering the profession. It was the initial screen. Students who could not successfully complete their professional studies could not be admitted into the profession. Once this point was reached, the schools had the obligation to graduate sufficient numbers of students to fill the needs of the professions. There was no other way.

This achievement had a tremendous effect on the quality of the professions. Educational requirements were written into law, and those persons with the high educational achievements were rewarded. Although the door into the professions was technically left ajar by the magic words "degree or equivalent" used in eligibility standards, most professions drew almost all of their entrants from the schools. Since the schools refused to graduate incompetent students, the quality of the professions rose rapidly. This effect can be seen in medicine, dentistry, and teaching. It grew directly out of the aim of the professional school to provide qualified entrants, and to provide them in sufficient numbers to meet the needs of society and the professions.

The aims of professional education are therefore two—to provide qualified entrants and to provide enough entrants. They may appear to be in conflict at times, since a program to provide enough graduates may ignore standards of quality for entrants. Under the present patterns of professional education, however, neither can be ignored.

The Aim of Sufficient Quantity

How large a group of the total work force in the United States falls under the term *professional?* Estimates vary, but according to the 1950 census data and later estimates professional workers account for from between 6½ and 10 per cent of the work force. By 1970, the estimates are that professional workers will constitute nearly 13 per cent of the work force, which itself will have increased from about 65 million in 1957 to 81.2 million.[2] From 6.5 million in 1957, the number of professional workers is expected to climb to about 10.4 million, an increase of nearly 4 million or nearly 60 per cent in thirteen years. If the professional schools are to come anywhere near to meeting the needs inherent in these estimates and requirements, a stupendous task lies before them. It is not certain that the schools will rise to it or will receive the support necessary for them to do so. Much of the stimulus for federal funds for higher education comes from these projections, since the universities and professional schools see no other method to acquire the finances.

The task will be difficult at best, perhaps insuperable. Almost every profession is plagued with shortages. Each wants more qualified entrants than it now receives. For example, the Engineers' Joint Council has expressed its "concern over the steady decline in U.S. engineering enrollments, in the face of an accelerating output of Soviet graduates."[3] In 1961, when Raymond J. Nagle, Dean of the School of Dentistry at New York University, was president of the American Dental Association, he stated flatly that "there has been a dropping, both in quality and quantity, in applications for admission to our dental schools."[4] The *Journal of the American Medical Association* reported a "widespread concern because of the decreasing numbers of qualified students who apply for admission to medi-

[2] *A Fact Book on Higher Education* (Washington, D.C.: American Council on Education, 1958), p. 146.

[3] The Engineering Research Committee, *The Nation's Engineering Research Needs 1965–1985* (New York: Engineers' Joint Council, Inc., 1962), Foreword.

[4] Raymond J. Nagle "Presidential Address," *Proceedings of the Thirty-Eighth Annual Session of the American Association of Dental Schools* (Chicago: American Association of Dental Schools, 1961), p. 9.

cal school."[5] In the same year, the National Education Association commented that "no sign of relief in the teacher shortage is in sight."[6] It is incontestable that the professions are not getting enough entrants now. Can there be much hope that they will in 1970 when the needs are expected to be 60 per cent greater?

The schools are making a strenuous effort to meet the demands. At present, about two-thirds of the bachelor's and first degrees awarded in the United States are given in professional fields, nearly one-fourth in teaching alone. The newer professions have surpassed the old to such an extent that medicine accounts for only about 2 per cent of the degrees and theology for only about 2.5 per cent. Much of the expansion of the professional schools therefore has been in the younger professional fields, and a considerable part of future expansion will be there also.[7]

The demands of a field like public school teaching, for example, increased directly with the increase in birthrate which began after World War II. In addition, longer training was required. Fifty years ago, the normal school with its two years of teacher training was all that the nation expected of teachers. Now a universal requirement of four years of college training for all public school teachers is nearly in sight, while the master's degree is widely required for secondary school teachers. Both better trained teachers and more teachers are needed.

Every profession is looking for additional entrants. The schools, under their obligation to satisfy the needs of the professions, are recruiting students. But the shortages continue and, in some fields, the number of applicants is declining. What can be done?

It is possible to do a number of things, but four appear to be essential. They are:

1. Persuade more qualified students to apply for entrance into professional schools.
2. As the numbers of students increase, establish schools to take care of them.
3. If possible, shorten the length of training.

---

[5] "Student Recruitment Activities," *Journal of the American Medical Association*, Vol. 178, No. 6 (November 11, 1961), 595.

[6] Ray C. Maul, "Highlights of 1962 Supply-Demand Report," *TEPS Newsletter* Vol. 5, No. 4 (May, 1962), 1.

[7] See the discussion contained in C. Lester Anderson, *et al., Education for the Professions* (Chicago: University of Chicago Press, 1962), pp. 4–13.

4. Organize the profession so that more ancillary and subprofessional personnel can be used under the supervision or guidance of the trained professionals.

Each of these suggestions, if diligently followed, may contribute to reducing the shortages which now hamper the professions in their efforts to serve society.

Recruiting students.   Almost every field is attempting to recruit more students. Professions use a variety of methods, all designed to make the practice of the profession seem more attractive and the course of entering it less burdensome. Professions with chronic shortages, such as nursing, teaching, and social work, have undertaken national programs of advertising and information to acquaint prospective students with the pleasures and profits of entering those professions. Information on salaries, working conditions, functions, and benefits is disseminated through radio and television programs, magazine articles, newspaper advertisements, and other means. Films, speakers, and pamphlets are available to secondary schools, and the guidance counselors, who have the opportunity of encouraging able students to choose professions, are bombarded with information.

The impact of the national campaigns apparently has some force. The Council on Social Work Education believes that its national recruitment efforts reversed the downward trend of enrollments, since the number of social work students has increased each year since the national efforts began. Others do not have as clear evidence, but they are sufficiently convinced to allot time and money to the programs.

Scholarships are a special form of recruiting. More scholarships of various sorts are becoming available to students in the professions. Oddly enough, they are less well established for the older professions than for the newer. Over four-fifths of social work students, for example, receive some kind of grant or scholarship during enrollment in schools of social work. Yet medical students receive relatively little help from scholarship funds, even though their period of training is longer and more expensive than that of the social worker. Scholarships and loan funds aid bright high school graduates whose funds are too limited to allow them to go on to college. These are the students toward whom many a scholarship program is aimed, including the National Merit Scholarships. These programs are supported by industrial and foundation funds, and the loan program is listed under the National Defense Education Act.

Scholarship programs have the particular function also of channeling high quality students into fields they might otherwise ignore. Scholarships of the Atomic Energy Commission, for example, were set at a much higher figure than normal university scholarships, with the intent of attracting young scientists to the newer fields of physics and chemistry that relate to nuclear energy. In fact, some medical educators complain that these scholarships and those of the National Science Foundation, reduced the number of able students who in other days would have entered medicine. Certainly money has helped to expand graduate programs by supporting students through the lengthened period of education.

As the demands for professional people increase and the competition for students grows keener, the professional schools are reaching into the high schools to encourage students to make their occupational choices at that time. Student clubs, like the Future Teachers of America, draw students into a quasi-official relationship with a profession and aid them in selecting the needed courses for later use in entering the professional schools. Summer work offered in the profession may also attract adherents. Professional schools, like industry, have been sending representatives to visit colleges and high schools in the hope of attracting stellar students. The ways of seduction are many.

Increasing the number of schools. If recruitment efforts can attract enough students, shortages in the professions can be alleviated by establishing new professional schools for them. As numbers of college students increase, the number of students who wish to enter professional schools will grow, but no one knows by how much. Most arguments for increasing the number of schools have rested on projections of need rather than on predictions of the numbers of students who will want to enter professional schools. Nevertheless, the number of graduates must be increased greatly merely to maintain the present ratios of practitioners to population. The expected increases in population are not fanciful. More people will need to be served by the professions. To do so, more graduates will be required. To obtain more graduates, more schools will be needed. So runs the argument.

This argument has significant force. Consultants to the Public Health Service have recommended that the nation establish some twenty new medical schools between now and 1970, merely to keep up with population increases. Seven universities—Arizona, Brown, California, Connecticut, New Mexico, Rutgers, and Texas —have announced plans to establish new two- or four-year schools, representing about a third of the requirement. Other fields are planning significant though less substantial expansion.

Reducing the length of training. Shortages could possibly be reduced by compressing the length of training. Doing so would attract students who now hesitate to enter a long and expensive course of training. Also, shortening the training would reduce the number of dropouts, who leave because of emotional fatigue or inadequate funds. Furthermore, shortening training would increase the years of practice. In spite of all these possibilities, the trends are in the other direction. Professional schools have lengthened training in the face of shortages. Medical education in some specialties now stretches over fourteen post-high school years. Many dental schools require four undergraduate years of study instead of the two established by national standards, making dentistry an eight-year post-high school course. Only a few professional schools have made any serious effort to reduce the length of training.

Establishing hierarchies of competence. Efforts to recruit additional students, to add new schools, and to shorten the length of training will not be sufficient to end the shortages. A fourth method, that of correlating training more closely to job requirements, will be necessary also. Several professions are doing their best to supplement the work of the trained professional person with the assistance of auxiliary persons who have shorter training and less skill. Engineering, for example, expects to need three to four engineering technicians for each engineer, thereby multiplying the usefulness of the engineer, and recruiting into engineering a number of persons who would not otherwise be able to qualify for it.

Nursing is using several training plans, including vocational school-hospital training for practical nurses, the two-year college program for registered bedside nurses, the three-year hospital training program also for registered nurses, the four-year bachelor's degree college program for head nurses, and the five-year master's degree program for supervisors and instructors. To some extent, each of these programs attracts its own clientele so that the number of trained nurses has increased as the programs have multiplied. The graduates of these programs are intended to fit the needs of the positions to which they go, without being undertrained or overtrained. Such a millenium is beyond hope, but the effort represents a unique attempt to rationalize training for a profession.

Medicine uses a great variety of personnel to assist the physician, many of whom have no training comparable to that of a physician. At least three of these assisting groups are thought of as professions in their own right—nursing, pharmacy, and hospital administration. Experiments in the practice of dentistry have shown that one dentist can double his output by employing a dental hygienist and a dental assistant. No one knows how far this can be pushed. The Public Health Service is undertaking a new series of experiments to determine whether a dentist can profitably use *four* assistants.

These changes in the organization of the professions cannot be accomplished without effort and pain. Social work and teaching have yet to accept the concept that assistants of various sorts can increase the usefulness of a professional person. Each of these professions is so convinced that the relationship with client or pupil must be infused with the personality of the professional person that it cannot be persuaded to look honestly at the usefulness of subprofessional assistance.

There are simply not enough professionals to go around. Social work will never obtain enough social workers through its present programs of two-year master's degrees. Four-fifths of all social workers, or some 83,000, do not hold the required two-year master's degree, but the schools at present graduate only about 2500, hardly enough to replace the social workers who leave the profession, let alone care for any expansion of population. Shortages will continue to plague the profession, no matter how much recruiting it does, unless it is willing to use more subprofessional persons with undergraduate training. Its present educational policy has the unreality of Alice's Wonderland. It is encouraging, though, that the Council of Social Work Education included undergraduate education in its curriculum study, and employed a staff specialist in undergraduate education. It may be emerging from the "looking glass." Teaching may possibly emerge also.

Principles for professional education suggested by the aim of sufficient quantity. ' Some principles can be derived from the preceding discussion. They are:

1. When professional schools obtained a monopoly for qualifying entrants for the professions, they also assumed the obligation of supplying enough entrants.
2. Members of the profession and the professional schools must cooperate to assure sufficient numbers of students in the schools.
3. All feasible methods, including reorganization of the ways professional services are provided, should be tried in order to help offset the shortages which plague the professions and therefore the society which they serve. The place of the professions is seriously threatened by shortages which require society to turn to nonprofessionals for the services it requires.

The Aim of Sufficient Quality

Professional schools cannot be satisfied merely with supplying sufficient "bodies" to staff the professions. Their graduates must be able to discharge the duties of the professions with success. Their performance must be more effective than the performance of persons with less training; otherwise the time, money, and energy invested in the programs of the schools could not be justified. A professional school has the obligation of constantly improving the performance of the profession within the limits of available funds. It tries, therefore, to increase the quality of graduates steadily so that society can be better served.

These ends are almost axiomatic. They are inherent in the concept of a professional school as the source of entrants for the professions. But when definition is pushed further, when lay persons or even professional educators ask what qualities the effective professional person must have, the answer becomes difficult. Difficult or not, an answer is needed. No education is possible without a definition of the criteria of its success. Its objectives must be defined before its direction can be determined. What are the desirable skills and attitudes that a professional person should be able to command?

Professional competence. A primary objective of professional education is to help its students obtain the knowledge and competence which are peculiar to the field. Education must help a prospective teacher to learn what and how to teach; a prospective surgeon to learn when and how to perform surgery; a prospective architect to learn how to design a building; a prospective engineer how to build a bridge or devise a machine; a prospective attorney how to prepare a brief. Each of these actions is a complex one, but they are all based on the competence which is peculiar to the profession.

Educators and practitioners can agree that graduates of the schools should be able to demonstrate that they are competent practitioners when they enter the profession. But the word "competence," like the word "excellence," is much too broad and amorphous to be a guide to the schools. In fact, practitioners and educators do not agree on the definition of "competence." They agree that it means the ability to execute tasks with a minimum of energy. They probably agree that it means the ability to solve problems with imagination and ingenuity even when the problems have novel elements and are not susceptible to textbook solutions. But educators and practitioners would probably disagree on what the tasks are and what specific competencies are required.

In general, the educators prefer to focus their attention on preparing the student for problems which he will reach after the initial stages of his career have been completed. Some practitioners, on the other hand, hold that the school should prepare the students to begin their work immediately after graduation, with little time for further learning and little opportunity for correcting mistakes. Such an attitude is justified in professions like medicine and dentistry, where the graduate will be called upon to conduct his practice almost without supervision. Such a profession asks that the training be lengthy, and that the school expose the student to situations which approximate the conditions under which he will later practice. Medicine requires the student to complete two years of clinical instruction in a medical school in which he learns the arts of practice, preferably in a hospital owned and operated by the medical school itself. Beyond that, the profession of medicine requires the student to complete at least one year of clinical training in the internship before it is willing to allow him to practice. If he is to become a specialist, he must undergo three to five more years of training, again largely in a clinical setting, not in a professional school. Dental students work in the dental clinic throughout their last two years to master the beginning skills of practice. Several other professions make this effort also—nursing, social work, teaching, veterinary medicine. Engineering, law, and business do less. The "cooperative system" in engineering under which students alternate sessions of campus study with sessions of off-campus work in industry has the same intent. Law simulates legal practice through its moot courts, and in a few schools business students are required to work with local firms during the school year.

The fact remains, however, that educators and practitioners disagree on the amount of practical experience the professional education should provide. The educator admits that some clinical experience is needed, but he wants the student to obtain the knowledge underlying the field he intends to enter rather than specific skills which may be needed at a single point in time. The educator is more concerned with principles and concepts than with skills and manuals. He believes that the student must master the theoretical assumptions and formulations he will be working with for most of his life, a life which, incidentally, will probably extend into the next century.[8] The educator is more likely to be concerned with preparing the student for high professional responsibilities than he is with teaching the skills of early practice. The educator places a value on knowledge; the practitioner on early competence. Both are needed.

Understanding of society. Students in professional education must become competent in their professions. Unless this is accomplished, nothing is gained. But the usefulness of competence may be sharply limited unless the student is able to place his skills within the context of society. A physician, for example, is affected by many nonmedical forces. The insurances support medical care for many who once could not afford it. Other professions and occupations join him as he practices within hospitals and public health agencies. Government undertakes tasks which were formerly left to private choice. In all these areas, he will need much more than competence in the practice of medicine. He must anticipate the directions in which society will move and make certain that within

---

8 See, for example, Rene J. Dubós, "Adaptability for Survival and Growth" in *Values and Ideals of American Youth*, Eli Ginzberg, ed. (New York: Columbia University Press, 1961). Dubós says, "The only knowledge of permanent value is theoretical knowledge, and the broader it is the greater are the chances that it will prove useful in practice because it is applicable to a wider range of conditions." p. 12.

the changed conditions of new social organization his contribution can continue to be made with skill and success.

Those professions which grow out of the social sciences—law, psychology, social work, and teaching, for example—must also relate their fields to social understanding. The understanding which a teacher obtains in professional courses must be broadened sufficiently to make sure that she, too, sees the school as a social agency, sometimes of change, sometimes of conservation. As a social agency, the school will shift in function from time to time. If the age distribution of the population changes, the cost of providing schools may rise because the number of children will increase, and it may require that teaching methods be adapted to larger groups of students. Because every social institution must continue to elicit support or lose its vitality, the teacher has an obligation to help the constituency of the school understand what is occurring.

It might be expected that social work, by its title, would be a profession in which students would almost automatically obtain social understanding. A social worker cannot help people to become independent and effective members of society without knowing a good bit about the society of which they are a part. But the literature of social work is full of complaints that social workers are so immersed in the problems of individual clients that they cannot effectively propose and support remedial legislation or social action which, if taken, would solve or ameliorate a great number of the cases with which they are so laboriously concerned. Without better understanding of the possibilities and limitations of social change, social work cannot make its full contribution to society.

Thus, the practitioner in every profession needs social understanding to do his work well. He needs it even in the introductory phases of his practice to provide a framework within which he can accumulate and interpret the experience he gains. He needs it to relate his practice to the larger social issues which face the profession and its society. It becomes increasingly important as the practitioner grows in influence and stature, for his actions begin then to affect many more people than simply those with whom he comes in contact. As an officer of his professional association or as a supervisor of other professional people, he must make sure that his actions are infused with a vivid understanding of their impact on society and their implications for the people in it. He cannot ignore the possible consequences of what he does, for as he arrives at positions of leadership he will determine the directions the profession will follow. Unless he understands the society about him, he can damage it and the profession unwittingly. If he knows the structure and dynamics of society, he can guide his profession with intelligence and wisdom.

Ethical behavior. Professional education must help its students to acquire competence and social understanding. It must also help students to value and demonstrate ethical behavior. It must so organize its educational experiences that the students will become imbued with the ethic of the profession and will throughout their lives guide their conduct by the principles of that ethic. Professional education has as much responsibility to help its students adopt ethical practices and principles as the basic guide of their future practice as the natural scientists have to make certain that their students follow the procedures of the scientific method in conducting research. The ethic which the scientific method incorporates—pursuit of truth, objectivity, dedication to discovery, submission of results to criticism by colleagues—is central to the concerns of physical science, and a student who shows himself unable to guide his research by it is properly prevented from becoming a scientist. In almost exact analogy, a student in a profession who is unable or unwilling to value the ethical principles of his profession should be prevented from entering—ever. Universally, the professions expect ethical behavior from their members. Universally, then, the professional school must do what it can to assure ethical behavior among its graduates.

This obligation is established in various ways, especially by the character of professions. All professions have one characteristic in common—ethical or altruistic behavior. The professions are set apart from other occupations because the professions have an ethic. Their members must practice so that their patients or clients —not themselves—receive the primary benefit. Without the dedication which such an ethic implies, a profession would disappear. In the catechism of the professions, exploitation of clients is a sin which lies beyond forgiveness.

The professions emphasize their profound concern with ethical behavior by stating their principles in codes. J. Bronowski, author of *Science and Human Values,* states:

> Every profession has its solemn codes: the lawyers and the salesmen, the accountants, the musicians and the consulting engineers. When a member of these combinations behaves outrageously, he is expelled. . . . And yet we have only to see how much alike are all these codes, how pious and how general, to know at once that they do not spring from the pith and sap of the work they regulate. They are not thrust up, a sharp green bough, from the ruling passion of their adherents. It is the other way about: their codes are a reminder to each profession that the sanctions of society at large reach into them also.[9]

It is not necessary to agree with Mr. Bronowski about the origin of the codes to recognize that the professions would be lost without them. The professions must live up to the codes as fully as it is humanly possible or face the probability that society will so alter their freedom that they cannot effectively practice. The monopoly which a profession enjoys is based on its guarantees of ethical behavior. With these guarantees, the professions are awarded a status which few other groups in a democracy can boast.

Professions place their codes and ethical principles at the center of their concern about themselves. The professions demonstrate their adherence by enforcing the codes, even to the point of expelling members who violate the codes "outrageously." In the United States in 1961, for example, state boards of medical examiners, largely composed of physicians, revoked 102 licenses, thereby depriving those members of the right to practice.[10] Many others must have been reprimanded by local medical societies for conduct thought to be contrary to the code. Other professions, like law, have equally severe methods of removing the right to practice from the serious offender.

Since ethical behavior is of surpassing importance to the professions, it must be an objective of professional education. It joins competence and social understanding as a third objective of professional schools.

Scholarly concern. Competence in practice, social understand-

---

[9] J. Bronowski, *Science and Human Values* (New York: Harper & Row, Publishers, Harper Torchbook edition, 1959), pp. 76–77.
[10] "Licenses Revoked," *New Medical Materia,* Vol. 4, No. 10 (October, 1962), 42. State boards took 604 disciplinary measures against doctors in 1961.

ing and ethical behavior are commonly accepted objectives of professional education. One last objective is equally important—to stimulate students and later practitioners to continue to study after graduation and to be able to conduct or interpret research. It is these attributes which makes the professions "learned," in the sense meant by Flexner. By this criterion he excluded many of the occupations which are now considered professions. He asked:

> How are we to distinguish professions that belong to universities from vocations that do not belong to them? The criteria are not difficult to discern. Professions are, as a matter of history—and very rightly—"learned professions"; there are no unlearned professions. Unlearned professions—a contradiction in terms—would be vocations, callings, or occupations.[11]

Dr. Flexner may have been thinking solely of the lengthy training which a profession requires to master its lore. But he may also have been thinking that a practitioner needs to continue learning far beyond the end of professional school so that he can absorb knowledge as it becomes available through research. No one man can hope to be master of all knowledge, but he has a professional obligation to try to keep abreast of those portions which are essential to his practice. He cannot do so without continued reading and study. The knowledge he acquires in professional school may be sadly out-of-date long before he reaches retirement. He must not run the risk of subjecting his patients or clients to the dangers of obsolete knowledge. He must continue to be a scholar, even in the press of practice.

Professional education should have the objective of helping him see and feel that his graduation is not the end of study. His zest for learning should increase as his focus of life sharpens upon his professional concerns. He may need to learn about fields of knowledge that were hardly in existence at the time he entered the profession. A professional person is a lifelong learner. His formal education permits him to enter the profession and his continuing education, largely guided by his own efforts, permits him to rise in his profession.[12]

---

[11] Abraham Flexner, *Universities: American, English, German* (New York: Oxford University Press, 1930), p. 29.

[12] For a strong statement of this aim, see H. Richard Niebuhr, *et al.*, *The Advancement of Theological Education* (New York: Harper and Row, Publishers, 1957), p. 209. *"The greatest defect in theological education today is that . . . it offers too little challenge to the student . . . to become an independent, lifelong inquirer. . . ."*

At the very least, his scholarly concern requires that he continue to study. But it may carry him much further. His professional education should qualify him to undertake research as time and opportunity permit. If he understands the methods in which research may be initiated and in which useful observations can be made, he will find satisfaction in trying to discover his own solutions to problems. A profession in which every member combined practice with some research, however minor, would be alert, skeptical, and informed. It would not be diverted by fads or encrusted with custom. Its contributions would continue to be fresh with the delights of discovery.

Not every member of a profession has the inclination or time to undertake the often tedious tasks of original research. But the professional school should make very sure that its graduates are competent to interpret research, to understand its methods and significance, to assess its findings, and to adopt those which have value. Even without conducting research, a professional person can obtain the results of research and make them available to society. His obligations to his learned profession are discharged by his willingness to study and his capacity to interpret research results, even though he executes no research projects himself.

These four objectives compose the aims of "qualified practitioner." To repeat, they are competence in practice of the profession, social understanding, ethical behavior, and scholarly concern. When the professional school focuses on these aims, it hopes that its graduates will enhance and expand their competence, social understanding, ethical behavior, and scholarly concern throughout their careers. These aims are not reached, therefore, at a single point in time. The school must judge itself and be judged on its influence over the full careers of its graduates. Nothing less than endless growth can be considered success.

Needs of professions vary. These objectives are common to the aim of quality in every profession, but each profession must define them in terms of its own requirements since each profession has knowledge and skill different from the others. A school teacher needs to know some elementary biology, if he expects to understand the growth patterns of the children placed in his care. A physician, however, must know human biology so thoroughly that he can successfully interfere with its functioning when such interference is necessary to produce health. A social worker must know, in general, the laws relating to adoption, for example, but the attorney must be able to use these laws in court procedures and in drafting documents which will withstand court test. His task is different from that of the social worker.

Similarly, each profession must define its needs in social understanding, where the general elements may be similar but the particulars will vary widely. Ethics, in the sense of concern for the welfare of client or patient, will be similar among professions, but a cursory study of the codes will show how greatly the particulars vary here also.[13] Finally, the kinds of research and continued study which each profession expects of its initiates will vary as considerably as the type and amount of knowledge which they are expected to master.

The aim of quantity, or sufficient numbers, and the aim of quality, or sufficient competence, may seem contradictory. To some extent they are, especially during periods of shortage. There is a constant temptation to reduce the requirements of education merely to increase the number with some training. These are not wise solutions, although in times of great emergency, like war, they can be used extensively and effectively. A medical corpsman was sufficient in battle to deal with first aid for the wounded, but he did not attempt to operate on shattered bodies. That was left for the surgeon. Regardless of emergency, a minimum of competence is essential to the professional task.

Keeping the aim of quantity in mind, however, can offset a profession's tendency to seek status by becoming so exclusive that it cannot execute its functions, with the result that the public turns to other less-qualified persons for help. A profession, on the one hand, can lose its usefulness by raising its entrance standards so high that students turn to other fields. On the other hand, inadequate training can destroy a profession in short order, particularly as a better-educated public learns what to expect of the properly-trained practitioner. In medicine, dentistry, and law, among other professions, the growth of the specialist reflects the public's insistence on receiving aid from those who are best qualified to give it.

---

[13] "Ethical Standards and Professional Conduct," *The Annals of the American Academy of Political and Social Science,* Vol. 297 (January, 1955). The issue contains articles on ethical standards in public accounting, architecture, medicine, law, engineering, three varieties of ministry, and public school teaching.

Thus, professional education represents a moving equilibrium formed by the opposing forces pushing toward the aim of quantity and the aim of quality in its graduates. Conflict between the aims must be resolved. There must be enough graduates to satisfy the needs of the professions, but these graduates must have sufficient competence to discharge their functions with success. Between these two aims professional education is shaped.

Principles for quality. A professional school which wishes to develop an educational program of high quality must follow certain principles. These have been suggested in the preceding discussion and are summarized here.

1. Professional education should be directed toward significant objectives including professional competence, understanding of society, ethical behavior, and scholarly concern.

2. A professional school should periodically review its procedures and programs and make such modifications as are needed to assure that they are contributing fully to movement toward the objectives.

3. Each of the objectives given above is valid, but professional schools have been more accustomed to emphasizing professional competence than the others. Additional effort should be placed on the other objectives to increase the quality of programs.

4. A program of professional education cannot ignore either the aim of quantity or the aim of quality. It must establish a moving equilibrium between them, but it cannot allow quality to drop below an essential minimum.

CHAPTER IV

The Problem of the Curriculum

The aims of professional education control its content. Such a flat statement does little, however, to define the many issues which swirl about the curriculums of professional schools. Every field is in a state of flux. None is wholly satisfied with the content it includes. Knowledge has exploded, but the professional man must master at least the essential parts of that knowledge or run the risk of being inadequate in practice. Choices must be made, for the professional educator must construct a curriculum which he believes is the most significant for the budding professional man. Furthermore, he must select only those parts which the professional school can best supply, leaving the rest to continued study and experience.

Also, a professional educator must choose on some consistent basis so that the curriculum has cohesion and importance. He will either be more concerned with theory than with skill, more with the processes of learning how to learn than with imparting knowledge of current affairs, or more concerned with the future than the present, although he will be concerned with the present also.

Content of the Curriculum

The issues of curriculum content grow largely out of the limitations on time. They concern: (1) basic arts and sciences vs. professional sciences and application; (2) professional sciences vs. application; and (3) principles vs. information. Each of the issues warrants attention.

Underlying these issues is an inclusive concept of the curriculum of professional education. Given the objectives of professional competence, social understanding, ethical behavior, and scholarly concern, the professional curriculum cannot be limited to those knowledges and skills that are precisely fitted to the requirements of a particular task. If that were all that the professional curriculum were expected to contain, the professional school need not find a home in the university. It could pursue its single-minded task in isolation, undiverted by other interests of intellect or attitude.

Professional educators have adopted a broader aim than mere competence to execute defined tasks. Notice how far the objectives extend. They include social understanding which can be gained partly through experience, but which also must be learned through the social sciences and humanities. They include ethical conduct, which requires not only understanding of the code of the profession, but an understanding of the history of mankind with its rise toward a civilized world in which the aim of fellowship and altruism has at least as much power as the aim of exploitation. Ethical conduct cannot be attained merely through conforming to a set of rules. It must be based on philosophical understandings concerning the meaning of existence and the character of man if it is to guide a practitioner through the brambles of practice. And the objectives include the elements of scholarly concern, with expectation of continued study and the advance of knowledge through research. Each of these objectives could be contained within a professional school, but once it contained them, it would assume the character of a university.

The point is very simple. What is taught in the professional school itself comprises only one part of the professional curriculum. On the one side, the professional curriculum includes the arts and sciences usually taught in the college of arts and sciences, often as a prerequisite to entrance into the professional school itself. On the other side, the curriculum includes the early years of practice under guidance and supervision, when the student is mastering the arts of application, not in the professional school. In between these parts stands the work of the professional school itself, devoted mainly to the professional sciences and the beginnings of application under carefully supervised or simulated conditions. These three parts constitute the whole of the professional curriculum—the arts and sciences, the professional sciences, and the skills of application. Any concept of the professional curriculum which is of less scope than this is inadequate and misleading.

It is necessary to understand that the three parts of the professional curriculum are ordinarily controlled by different groups. The college of arts and sciences usually provides instruction in the basic arts and sciences, even when the student is enrolled in the professional school during his undergraduate period, and always when he is to enter the professional school after a period of college study. Also, much of the instruction which a student will receive in the arts of application follows his graduation from the professional school. It is given by an industry, an institution, or a hospital which is located outside of the university or professional school. Cooperation between the professional school and the college of arts and sciences, on the one hand, and between the professional school and the agencies of practice, on the other, is essential to effective programs of professional education. Without cooperation, the three parts of the professional curriculum could sunder, leaving the baffled student to put them back together. At times, he is forced to do just that. He suffers in having to do so.

Professional sciences is not a common term. As used in this volume, the term designates the parts of one science or the grouping of parts of several sciences which have pertinence to the work of the profession. In medicine, the *professional sciences* are largely human biology—physiology, anatomy, biochemistry, biophysics, pathology—and fields which affect human biological functioning, such as microorganisms (microbiology) and drugs (pharmacology). None of these so-called basic medical sciences deals with anything but human biology. All ignore plant and animal biology, except as these may have usefulness in the human biology. Anatomy is concerned with the anatomy of the human body, not with the anatomy of any other animal or with any plant. Pathology is the result of malfunctioning of human biology. In fact, the term *basic medical sciences* should have the emphasis placed on the word *medical*. *Basic* must be interpreted to mean "basic to medicine" rather than basic in the sense that chemistry is basic to the study of all sorts of organic and inorganic substances.

What medicine calls the *basic medical sciences* is precisely what the term *professional sciences* is intended to convey. Engineering uses the term *engineering sciences* in the way that *professional sciences* is used here. Engineering is referring to knowledge derived from the basic sciences of physics, chemistry, and mathematics, and focused on the functions of engineering. Fluid mechanics is an engineering science, derived from the physics of liquids, but is a more intensive study than an introduction to physics would contain. In most cases, the basic sciences are a part of the responsibility of the college of arts and sciences, the professional sciences a part of the professional school.[1]

The term *application* is more familiar than *professional sciences*. It means the process of combining the knowledge and skill learned in the college of arts and sciences and the professional school and applying them to the solution of problems in the professional field. Without application, knowledge is inert.

The art of application may be explored in professional school, but its refinement inevitably comes with the experience of practice. If that practice is under supervision, as in an engineering or architectural firm, the school can transfer much of the responsibility to the profession itself. If, however, the graduate enters practice immediately in isolation, often having to accept full responsibility for his decisions, the school is forced to pay much greater attention to application before the student graduates. Thus, medicine and dentistry which are often practiced in isolation rather than under hierarchies of supervisors use virtually two years or one-half of the school period to develop skill in application—the *clinical years,* as they are called. Teaching requires students to spend considerable time with *professional laboratory experiences* to the same end. Social work and public health nursing students have extended opportunities to learn under supervision how they should apply their knowledge. They, too, will often practice with little moment-by-moment supervision once they enter their professions.

The relations between these parts of the curriculum and their relationship to the school, the college of arts and sciences, and the agency can be charted as indicated in Fig. 1 on the next page. Logically, the basic arts and sciences, the professional sciences, and application form a sequence, progressing from the more general to the more specific. Figure 1 underlies consideration of the content, the length, and the organization of the curriculum. It should be kept in mind during the ensuing discussion of the issues of content.

---

[1] The importance of the basic sciences and the professional sciences increases as new knowledge multiplies. In describing "The Art and the Science" of medicine, Dr. C. Sidney Burwell, Professor of Medicine Emeritus at Harvard, says: "The fact that today's students must prepare themselves for tomorrow's medicine gives added importance to experience in the basic medical sciences since by and large the future changes in medicine will be understood best by those who are competent in these basic sciences." *The Choice of a Medical Career,* Joseph Garland and Joseph Stokes III, eds. (Philadelphia: J. B. Lippincott Co., 1961), p. 1.

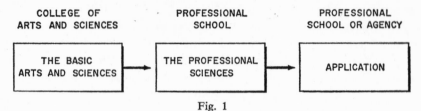

Fig. 1

Source and Relationships of Parts of Professional Curriculums

Basic arts and sciences vs. professional sciences and application. Because the length of the curriculum is limited, conflict between agencies responsible for its parts is probably inevitable. Each agency struggles for a larger share of the available time. The struggle for control of the curriculum surely antedates the medieval university, where the curriculum finally settled into the famous seven liberal arts—the trivium and the quadrivium, the trivium being composed of grammar, logic, and rhetoric, and the quadrivium of the mathematical sciences, arithmetic, geometry, astronomy, and music. Except in the form of logic, the philosophical bent of the Greek schools had disappeared, and except for astronomy, their interest in the sciences had departed. Even by the middle ages then, the curriculum had changed beyond anyone's expectation. The seven liberal arts themselves seem sharply constrained when compared with the courses offered by a college of arts and sciences today. There was no history or social science, no laboratory science at all, no languages. It was not until the Renaissance that these constrictions were removed.

⌐At present, the college of arts and sciences devotes more time to the development of knowledge and understanding than to occupational ends. It sometimes prides itself on its lack of immediate focus on "useful" purposes. It considers itself a place in which young minds can stretch and compare and assess and evaluate, always looking forward to the time when knowledge can support a sound sense of values around which a personal philosophy can be constructed.⌐

The development of an integrated human being whose actions and values are meshed is a matter of tremendous significance, not to be underrated by all the professional schools in the world. But some supporters of the college claim too much by implying that college study should have no vocational significance. It is not enough to arrive at a set of beliefs by which a life can be guided. That life must also have content through making contributions to society in certain specialized ways. Through the occupation, the individual becomes influential in the lives of others, and society benefits broadly.

At first glance, the objectives of the arts and sciences and of the professional sciences appear to be irreconcilable; but the professional man needs the contributions both of the college with its emphasis on understanding and integrity, and of the professional school with its emphasis on the solving of human problems through the application of knowledge. Through the college, a student may have the good fortune to learn what is worth doing; through the professional school he may have the good fortune to learn how to do it. The conflict would seem to be more apparent than real, for the value of both college and professional school is unmistakable.

In addition to being a place for exploration and development of a set of beliefs about man and his world, the college introduces the student to the knowledges which underly the later practice of the profession. It helps a student who expects to enter law to understand the concepts of sociology and the findings of anthropological research so that he may place law in its proper context of human concern. It helps a premedical student to obtain insights into chemistry, physics, and mathematics on which his later studies of the basic medical sciences will rest. It helps him also to explore the human spirit through literature, art, languages, and philosophy so that he never makes the error that man lives by health alone. These are contributions which can best be made by the college, because it can provide broader and deeper understandings of these areas than can be done in any but the largest of professional schools.

Although parts of professional curriculum can best be presented by the college of arts and sciences, conflict between the college and the professional schools over the amounts of time to be devoted to general education and to the professional sciences bubbles merrily. The college claims that what it teaches has a value greater than the professional sciences, which are derived, adapted, and limited by their focus on the needs of a profession. A college faculty sometimes implies that only the subjects it defines as "basic" are really necessary to the person who wishes to enter a profession. They may hold this view particularly for teacher education. They would have more difficulty in justifying such a position about the medical sciences or the engineering sciences. The issue is not usually stated in absolute terms, however. Most colleges of arts and sciences accept the fact that the professional sciences and their application are useful. They hold, however, that the undergraduate years should be spent in general studies without focus on a profession, leaving professional training to the years beyond the baccalaureate degree. Again the issue is stated most sharply

TABLE I

Proportions of Curriculums Devoted to Arts and Sciences,
Professional Sciences, and Application, by Fields

Field	Arts & Sciences		Professional Sciences		Application	
Architecture[2]	12	per cent	88	per cent	Three years after graduation	
Business[3]	40	per cent	60	per cent	————	
Dentistry	50	per cent	25	per cent	25	per cent
Engineering[4]	18	per cent	82	per cent	In "co-op" arrangements only	
Law	50	per cent	50	per cent	————	
Medicine	50	per cent	25	per cent	25	per cent
Nursing[5]	50	per cent	25	per cent	25	per cent
Social Work	66⅔	per cent	16⅔	per cent	16⅔	per cent
Teaching[6]	50	per cent	31	per cent	19	per cent
Vet. Medicine	33⅓	per cent	33⅓	per cent	33⅓	per cent

[2] Jennings B. Sanders, *General and Liberal Education Content of Professional Curricula: Architecture* (Washington, D.C.: Government Printing Office, 1955), p. 11.

[3] Standard 3, *Standards for Membership in the American Association of Collegiate Schools of Business* (St. Louis, Missouri: The Association, 1956).

[4] Jennings B. Sanders, *General and Liberal Education Content of Professional Curricula: Engineering* (Washington, D.C.: Government Printing Office, 1954), p. 12.

[5] Margaret Bridgman, *Collegiate Education in Nursing* (New York: Russell Sage Foundation, 1953), p. 143.

[6] L. H. Clark, "The Curriculum for Elementary Teachers in Sixty-eight State Teachers Colleges," *Journal of Teacher Education*, Vol. 6, No. 2 (June, 1955), 115.

in teacher education, where the Master of Arts in Teaching has been combined from four years of general education leading to a bachelor's degree and one year of professional sciences and application. (This plan has been identified with Harvard University, although it has been tried in a number of other places under the stimulus of Ford Foundation funds.)

To faculty members who consider that four years are too brief a time for general studies, any time used by the professional sciences and application is too much. Beyond that absolute position, there is little agreement about what proportions of general education and professional sciences and application are best. Each field has found different ways of dividing the years available to it. Some have lengthened the total curriculum so that the conflict is minimized. Roughly the fields follow the relationships indicated in Table I.

Dentistry, law, medicine, social work, clinical psychology, and veterinary medicine all require from two to four years of college before admission to the professional school. They absorb a smaller proportion of the undergraduate years than the fields which compete directly for college time. Studies made under the direction of Dr. Earl J. McGrath at Teachers College, Columbia University, demonstrate that the curriculum of the college of arts and sciences has been deeply affected by increased emphasis on preparation for the various professions, particularly the newer ones.[7] Colleges of arts and sciences themselves now offer some fifty professional and preprofessional curricula. In 1900, they offered only six. About two-thirds of the bachelor's and first degrees given in the United States are awarded in professional fields. There is obvious danger that the college of arts and sciences will become more and more of a professional school. Its offerings in the basic arts and sciences may be so compressed that they become superficial and cursory rather than penetrating and stimulating to further studies.

Of undergraduate programs, architecture and engineering devote the least time to general studies. The teaching curriculum has as large a proportion of basic arts and science courses as any of the other fields. Attacks on teacher education have charged that too

---

[7] Earl J. McGrath and Charles H. Russell, *Are Liberal Arts Colleges Becoming Professional Schools?* (New York: Teachers College, Columbia University, Bureau of Publications, 1958). Dr. McGrath and his colleagues have also made very interesting studies of individual professions which use parts of the undergraduate years of college.

much of the curriculum is devoted to professional subjects. It may be too much, but it is considerably less than the proportions devoted to professional subjects in a number of other fields.

Professional sciences versus application. The professional school sits like the god Janus, looking forward and back. It looks back to the college of arts and sciences where the student should master liberal arts subjects sufficiently to serve as the basis of social understanding, appropriate professional behavior, and scholarly interest. The professional school is not able to achieve these ends alone, but it does have the right and obligation to urge the college of arts and sciences to fulfill them. It can properly expect that students coming to it from the college will be familiar with the major concepts and attitudes of the arts and sciences. Often the college fails and the professional school is tempted to undertake the task itself. If it succumbs, it will probably warp the student's learning by pressing the subject matter to professional ends. It is better for students in the professions to explore the arts and sciences in the college, where the disciplines have their own place and status, than in the professional school where the disciplines may be skewed to meet what are considered to be the needs of the professional student. But like Janus the professional school also looks forward, past graduation to the time when the student enters his profession and assumes the responsibilities attendant thereto. His learning will not, and indeed cannot, stop after professional school. He must keep on learning throughout his professional life, but he cannot enter a profession without some skill in the art of application.

The professional school shares the area of application with the profession. In fact, in a number of fields, the student learns most of the art of application after he leaves the professional school. In engineering, for example, the school may find it impossible to include within the allotted time all the knowledge, skills, and attitudes which engineering requires of its entrants and still have enough of the four years left to do much toward helping students learn how to apply their knowledge to professional problems. The so-called "scientifically-oriented" engineering curriculum makes a virtue of this necessity. Its proponents found that both the engineering schools and industry preferred that the school time be devoted to the sciences as fully as possible, with a minimum left for application. The industries preferred to do the training in application and skills so that (1) the training could be up-to-date, and (2) the time of the professional schools could be saved for what they could best supply, i.e., instruction in the professional sciences.[8]

In general, those fields in which the entrants begin practice in fairly isolated circumstances expend the most time on application. Medicine, dentistry, social work, and veterinary medicine all spend as much time on application as they do on professional sciences. Law is an exception. Even though its graduates may enter practice on their own, the law school gives them very little help on the skills of application. There have been proposals for legal internships, but as yet these have not been systematically organized. Law graduates compete vigorously, however, for various law clerkships with Supreme Court and other judges as well as with experienced attorneys, recognizing that some years of supervised study of actual legal practice will be of benefit.

Teaching, architecture, and engineering give relatively smaller amounts of attention to the skills of application. In most teacher education programs, for example, only one semester out of the total of eight is devoted to practice teaching. In each of these fields, the young professional is likely to begin work under fairly close supervision and guidance, and the professional school has left much of the learning about application to these agencies. Some educators and employers are not satisfied with this arrangement, since it asks a noneducational agency to complete the educational task.

Concepts versus information.   Educators who organize the professional curriculum have a difficult task. No attorney is expected to know all the law. No teacher can possibly know all of the elements of his subject. A professional person cannot hope to master even all the knowledge which is pertinent to his field, and his knowledge of related fields is bound to be cursory at best. A physicist will often be lost at the oral examination of a Ph.D. candidate in chemistry, or even in another branch of physics with which he has had little recent contact. The professional person whose practice is related to several fields of knowledge has an even harder time.

This difficulty forces the professional school to concern itself with concepts and theory, with principles and general procedures, rather than with the impossible task of presenting all the information

---

[8] See American Society for Engineering Education, *Report of Evaluation of Engineering Education,* (Urbana, Illinois: The Society, 1955).

which research has supplied to the scientific fields. Its students must learn facts, for they must see how principles are derived from the facts at hand. They cannot, however, learn all the facts, and principles and procedures must continue to be tentative, embraced only for so long as the facts support them, and ruthlessly modified or discarded to meet the impact of new discovery or even of new concepts broadly adopted. The advent of penicillin and the other broad-spectrum drugs, for example, changed the general practice of medicine beyond recognition, and sharply modified the specialization of "ear, nose, and throat." Penicillin can be prescribed with as much likelihood of success by a general practitioner as by a specialist. Since penicillin attacks a number of diseases, the art of diagnosis decreases in importance.

If a succession of case studies indicates that the principle of the foster family is preferable to that of the orphanage, social work procedure must change its emphasis from trying to improve orphanages to trying to place children in foster homes. This change in principle incorporates hosts of facts whose interpretations establish the concept of maintaining the child in as nearly normal a family situation as possible. That principle becomes the basis of a new concept for social work which guides its future practitioners. They should never conclude, however, that the concept is immutable, if other facts suggest and support different concepts.

The task of the professional school, then, is to organize its curriculum by integrating concepts and principles. It must find ways of relating known facts so that they can support or overturn these concepts and principles. Students can be taught the process by which the fact becomes the principle and thereby guides practice. They can be shown also how practice must constantly guard against the rigidities of tradition and maintain the flexibility of a science. As they see these things, they will be prepared to face the consequences of new facts, and will be able to interpret them into new principles and procedures.

Principles relating to content.   From this discussion of content some general principles can be drawn as guides for curriculum-makers.

1. The content of the curriculum should reflect the aims of the professional education. Since these aims are broader than professional competence, the curriculum cannot be defined by job descriptions alone.

2. Because the objectives of professional education include such items as social understanding, ethical behavior, and scholarly concern, the content of the curriculum must include experiences that will be helpful in these directions.

3. The curriculum should be considered as the sum of exposures to the basic arts and sciences, the professional sciences, and the arts of application. Any curriculum that lacks one of these is inadequate.

4. Usually, the content of the curriculum, as just defined, requires that the college of arts and sciences, the professional school, and the practicing profession share responsibility for different aspects. It is essential, therefore, that the professional school obtain and keep the cooperation of the college of arts and sciences and of the profession.

5. Curriculum-makers for professional schools must be aware of new knowledge which is constantly being added to the fields on which the professions depend. They must be willing to derive from the new knowledge principles and concepts which will establish more effective practice.

6. The content of the professional curriculum should not attempt to do much toward teaching the tricks of the trade. Instead, it should attempt to do as much as it can to provide the understandings on which the practitioner can create his own methods, if he wishes. It is much more important for a teacher to know that there are wide differences among children in their intellectual and physical growth than it is to know that it is often helpful to group children in a reading class according to ability.

7. The content of the curriculum should not be so voluminous that it overwhelms the student. The purpose is to help develop a graduate who wishes to continue to study, not one who is turned away from it by the inordinate demands which the curriculum makes during his school years.

Length of the Curriculum

The length of the curriculum of the professional school is initially determined by the amount of content which it contains and therefore the time required for a student to master it. Other factors may also affect the length. Each profession is master of a body of knowledge peculiar to its practice. It may believe that the longer a student takes to learn that knowledge the more significant the profession becomes. This kind of status-seeking can be highly desirable, if it influences inadequately educated professions into longer study and greater competence. It is sometimes hard to believe that all lengthening is justified. But other professions look at the field of medicine. It has acquired status, and its training is lengthy. A profession seeking status begins to wonder whether it should lengthen the program of education its entrants undergo in order to raise its status. On the other hand, lengthening can be justified. Thus, the extension in training for nurses from three hospital years to four college years and beyond not only supplies nurses who are better able to enter supervisory positions, but also increases the status of nursing by basing entrance to it upon possession of an academic degree.

Most professional school curriculums have become longer in spite of continuing shortages of practitioners and faculty members. Medical schools have added a year usually by requiring four rather than three years of undergraduate work before admission to medical school, and schools of dentistry prefer four predental years when not long ago they required only two. Law continues to accept students after three years of undergraduate study but gives preference to students with four years of college.

At the other end, medicine has greatly increased the years of residency, now a prerequisite to specialized practice. Some residencies extend for five years, and the minimum is three. The prospect of becoming a surgeon seems interminable to the entering student—four years of college, plus four years of medical school, plus one year of internship, plus three years, at a minimum, of residency, stand between the eighteen-year old entering college and his goal of beginning to practice surgery. With military service, he is over thirty years old before he can begin to practice.

Some few efforts have been made to shorten the length of professional education but they have been sporadic. The School •of Medicine of the Johns Hopkins University plans to accelerate the training of a small group of unusually well-qualified students, admitting them to medical school at the end of their second undergraduate year. Nursing has advanced further by establishing the two-year community college program which leads to the associate in arts degree and eligibility for taking the state licensing examinations in several states. This program eliminates one year from the hospital programs and two years from the collegiate programs. It is designed to provide much the same training as the hospital program but with better planning and therefore with saving of time. It also has the advantage of being a college program which may attract women for whom the hospital program lacks appeal. Nursing has also tried to make practical nursing more attractive, condensing its curriculum into an eighteen-month training period, with a third of this time allowed for study in a vocational high school. The Veterinary Medical School at the A. and M. College of Texas has instituted a trimester program of forty-five weeks in which a student can complete work toward the degree in slightly less than three years instead of the usual four.[9]

On the other hand, clinical psychology has insisted that its practitioners be educated as research men, with the inevitable result that the Ph.D. degree which admits the clinical psychologist to practice requires four years or longer after undergraduate study is completed.

The length of curriculums should be determined by how long it takes to prepare someone to enter a particular profession and not by other factors, such as the relative status of professions. Professional schools must frequently review their curriculums with care and firmness to avoid merely adding new knowledge to the old and lengthening the curriculum until students and society rebel. Some medical students complain that the fourth year of medical school is largely wasted, and medical educators are doubting the usefulness of the year of internship in a time when residencies are becoming more common and clinical teaching begins in the third year of medical school. But reduce the medical school curriculum to three years? Stanford University has recently increased its program to five. The minimum length of the various programs of professional education can best be demonstrated by Fig. 2.

As Fig. 2 shows, there is little uniformity to the length of education required for the professions. The older professions of law, dentistry, and medicine do not require a bachelor's degree before entrance, but each gives preference to persons with that degree. Architecture and pharmacy have lengthened their curriculums to five years and provide a bachelor's degree to symbolize success. Teaching allows persons with bachelor's degrees to enter practice, but the better certificates and positions go to persons with advanced degrees so that a master's degree is virtually required for secondary school teaching in many systems and for elementary schools in some. These three fields have all, therefore, extended their curriculum by at least a year.

---

[9] See Editorial "More Veterinarians in Fewer Years," *Journal of the American Veterinary Medical Association,* Vol. 140, No. 8 (April 15, 1962), 825–826.

FIELD	1	2	3	4	5	6	7	8	9	10	11	12
AGRICULTURE	P	P	P	P								
ARCHITECTURE	P	P	P	P	P							
BUSINESS ADMINISTRATION	P	P	P	P								
DENTISTRY	A	A	P	P	P	P						
ENGINEERING	P	P	P	P								
FORESTRY	P	P	P	P	P							
HOME ECONOMICS	P	P	P	P								
LAW	A	A	A	P	P	P						
MEDICINE	A	A	A	P	P	P		I	R	R		
NURSING	P	P	P	P								
OPTOMETRY	P	P	P	P	P							
PHARMACY	P	P	P	P								
PSYCHOLOGY	A	A	A	A	P	P	I					
SOCIAL WORK	A	A	A	A	P	P						
TEACHING	P	P	P	P	P							
VETERINARY MEDICINE	A	A	P	P	P	P						

Fig. 2   KEY: COLLEGE OF ARTS AND SCIENCES
                       PROFESSIONAL SCHOOL
                       INTERNSHIP
                       RESIDENCY

Engineering is in a special category because its curriculum is so heavy that it now needs about four and a half years of study. It has firmly refused to extend the curriculum officially to five years, but it has in fact come close to doing so by the number of hours of work it requires.

Nursing and social work are fairly recent members of universities. They have adapted themselves to the university organization, but in different ways. Nursing entered seeking education which was broader and more advanced than it could obtain from the hospital school. It wanted this type of education for its supervisors and head nurses. It accepted the four-year curriculum and attempted to fill it with useful content, since it wanted a bachelor's degree to certify its accomplishment. On the other hand, as has been said, it has also established the two-year course to supply bedside nurses. These programs have been popular in public junior colleges. They supplement the hospital school and the baccalaureate programs.

Social work, in an historic decision made in 1937, concluded that nothing less than a two-year master's degree program would suffice. It based this program on four years of undergraduate work leading to a bachelor's degree, although it did not specify what subjects should be studied. It adopted the organization of the university, and insisted on graduate degrees for its students. By this decision, social work made it impossible to meet the needs for trained social workers, but it substantially increased the level of competence of the graduating social worker.

Principles of length. Although there is little uniformity in length of professional curriculums, it is possible to suggest certain principles as guides. They are:

1. Professions have considerable freedom in determining the length of their curriculums, and they arrive at very different conclusions on the length required to obtain beginning competence.

2. Ideally, the length of the curriculum should be determined by the time an average student would require to obtain the knowledge and skill and absorb the attitudes necessary for beginning practice and a base for future growth. In sad fact, other factors enter into the decisions—desire for status, unwillingness to discard or compress old material to make room for new, efforts to develop specialized skills on a uniform base, and others.

3. The new knowledge which research is constantly adding must often be incorporated into the curriculum, if the education is to be aimed at achieving competence. The length of the curriculum should never be considered final. It can be increased to incorporate new knowledge when necessary, and it can be reduced when more efficient methods of instruction are discovered or more graduates are needed.

4. Since the content of the curriculum is changing, the length should be studied to determine whether it must be modified along with the content.

5. The curriculum should be no longer than necessary to accomplish its objectives.

6. Lengthening any part of the curriculum lengthens the whole. To increase the time required for the basic arts and sciences, even though instruction in these is provided in the college rather than in the professional school, increases the length of the professional curriculum. In the same way, increasing the requirements subsequent to professional school

and prior to practice, also lengthens the curriculum as a whole, just as much as lengthening the curriculum taught by the professional school.

Organization of the Curriculum

Even after questions concerning the content and the length of the curriculum are decided, educators in the professions are faced with organizing the content so that it can be mastered with a minimum of unnecessary effort and a maximum of understanding. The purpose of curriculum organization is to make it as easy as possible to learn and retain as much as possible in as little time as possible. The criterion, then, is efficiency of learning.

Logic versus psychologic.   Not enough is known about the processes of learning for curriculum-makers to reach more than tentative conclusions about organization of the curriculum. The different fields have reached different conclusions. Some of the reasons are as much historical as scientific. The sharp division between the college of arts and sciences and the professional school is an historical fact based on their separate origins. In a number of fields, including medicine, dentistry, social work, veterinary medicine, and law, virtually all attention to the basic arts and sciences is completed before attention to any of the professional sciences begins. Engineering, on the other hand, tries to keep the two parts in a more nearly parallel course, although it too places the basic sciences before the professional sciences, since the latter derive from the former. The University of Florida proposed at one time to organize its medical school curriculum so that it dovetailed with the undergraduate curriculum, furnishing a two-four-two division, with the professional sciences of the medical school and the arts and sciences being parallel within the four-year central period. Such an organization would require students to choose medicine at the end of their sophomore year, but it would relate the basic arts and sciences to the medical sciences more effectively than the usual sequence.

Some decisions about organization are based neither on historical accident nor on hypotheses about learning. Instead, they are based on convictions about roles. Under this theory, the role of the college of arts and sciences is to allow students to explore all fields of knowledge as widely as they wish, unrestricted by the requirements of a profession or professional school. The part of the curriculum dealing with the basic arts and sciences must be completed before the professional sciences are begun. Social work, dentistry, clinical psychology, law, medicine, and often theology follow this concept.

The logic of completing the basic arts and sciences before undertaking the professional sciences has equal force in completing the professional sciences before beginning study of the arts of application. Logically, the three parts of the professional curriculum form a sequence. Where the three parts are organized in logical sequence, however, as they were in medicine throughout the country up to a very few years ago, certain difficulties appear. First, since the premedical student in the college of arts and sciences wishes to qualify for medical school, he takes only those subjects which he thinks will improve his chances of admission. He takes as many sciences and as few arts as possible. Instead of increasing the breadth of his study, organizing the two parts of the curriculum in sequence narrowed the scope of studies he otherwise would have followed. In the same way the medical student has such a desire to practice that he may look upon the first two years of professional sciences as subjects to be learned and forgotten once he reaches his real objective—the years of clinical training.

In this kind of situation, study of the professional sciences inevitably seems to postpone rather than hasten entrance into practice, and students are restless with the delay. They consider the professional sciences as subjects that must be endured but not understood, that must be acquired but hardly enjoyed.

If the sequence is altered in part, the interest of the student rises. When he sees practitioners at work, he can begin to see the need of the professional sciences in practice. Obviously, this objective calls for careful and imaginative supervision. If the student is provided with guidance, with a chance to discuss what he has seen, with an analysis of his reactions and understandings, he will quickly realize the need for professional sciences.

Some professions follow this "illogical" sequence entirely in the professional sciences and application. Instead of completing the study of professional sciences before undertaking the study of application, social work, for example, parallels its theoretical classroom instruction in the professional sciences with a nearly equal amount of field instruction which exposes the student immediately and directly to the practice of the profession. He brings the problems he encounters with him to seminars and conferences, where he discusses their meanings and solutions with faculty and fellow students. In engineering schools which function on the "cooperative plan," work in industry alternates with campus study in blocks of a quarter or semester each. Faculty members find that the student returning to the campus from his assignment in industry approaches his studies with considerably more interest and respect than he had when he left the campus.[10] Most "co-op" schools begin the alternation in the junior year, after the student has gained enough knowledge to be useful in his industry assignment.

Specialty versus synthesis. The organizational principle underlying the curriculum therefore shifts back and forth from the logical to the psychological, never completely resting at either extreme. It also shifts back and forth from emphasis on the specialties, the "disciplines," to emphasis on integration or synthesis of knowledge to make the knowledge useful in practice. Schools use research men as teachers, and the research interests of these teachers tend to determine the organization of the curriculum. Courses multiply, specialties increase, fields become narrower, until educators suddenly realize that the student must expend great effort to incorporate course information into a workable body of knowledge with little help from the faculty or the curriculum. At that point, the faculty should set up means of helping the student integrate or relate the knowledge he is gaining from the specialties.

The schools have found a number of means of integrating knowledge. The School of Medicine of Western Reserve University has organized its curriculum around organ systems rather than disciplines, with the result that a student may be considering the kidney with a biochemist, a physiologist, an anatomist, and a pharmacologist all at the same time. In like fashion, the social work student may be considering human growth and development with psychologists, psychiatrists, physicians, geneticists, sociologists, and anthropologists simultaneously in group teaching efforts. In fact, the rise of the "workshop" as a preferred method of in-service education for

---

[10] For this and a number of other interesting effects of the "cooperative plan," see James W. Wilson and Edward H. Lyons, *Work-Study College Programs* (New York: Harper & Row, Publishers, 1961).

adult students grows out of its facility in assembling a variety of disciplines to help students solve problems which they have found significant in professional practice.

Team teaching combines several specialties in one course and is therefore a means of correlating knowledge. The project method of the architects and engineers is another method. Projects are simulated problems of considerable complexity, in which the student is given a set of facts and asked to propose a defensible solution. To do so, the student draws knowledge from several disciplines in ways that make relationships clear. Law schools attempt much the same thing through moot courts, where facts are presented and argued within standard courtroom procedure.

A similar method is the *clinico-pathological conference* (CPC) of the medical schools. In a CPC, a student reviews the medical records of a case, reaches a tentative diagnosis, and then defends his conclusion before a group of faculty members, which usually includes the attending physician and the pathologist. When the student later takes on full responsibility for a case, he has had some experience in coordinating what he has learned.

Even without team teaching, the curriculum can be organized so that it is easier for the student to integrate knowledge. Part of the solution lies in timing. Related sciences can be considered at nearly parallel times. If a student investigates the physiology of the blood and the biochemistry of food absorption at about the same time, he can easily comprehend the significance of each for the other. In the same way, the study of neuroanatomy and neurophysiology at the same time will illumine each other.

Ultimately, integration in the professional school curriculum occurs with the work on the art of application, the third major division of the curriculum. In this division, the student, by identifying with his preceptor, by recall and use of principles learned throughout his previous study, and by accepting responsibility thrown upon him, chooses from what he has learned those bits of knowledge, concepts, and information which are germane to the situation before him, and adopts appropriate solutions for the difficulties the situation presents.

The process is too complex to detail here, and much of it is still unexplored. Charlotte Towle has brilliantly described the process as a personality change in her book, *The Learner in Education for the Professions.*[11] The point is that the student must bring to focus upon a problem all the skills and knowledge that he has acquired up to that time, and he must be able to combine them into an effective procedure that relieves the difficulty. His ability to integrate skill and knowledge in different combinations as required by the situation he faces is the ultimate achievement his education is designed to reach. Without that, both the student and the school have failed.

It is obvious, therefore, that the clinical teacher in medical schools and teaching hospitals, the supervising teacher in practice teaching, the field instructor in social work, and all the other preceptors which the professions use to demonstrate and transmit the art of application to their students have tremendous responsibilities. They can be effective teachers only if they are analytical about the disciplines which make up their own skills, and can point out these relationships to their students. They must be skilled at combining what they know in a variety of ways for different situations, always guided by an analysis of the situation and a choice of method to solve it. They must never propose solutions solely by formula, without being willing to show how the formula applies to a certain situation better than any other formulation could. Always, they must urge the students to try to locate the new and preferable solution, remaining eternally dissatisfied with an inadequate method no matter how hallowed with tradition it may have grown.

The art of application is not the following of cookbook recipes; it is the imaginative use of knowledge and skill to propose solutions not before attempted. It is the art of using skill and knowledge to unfasten the limits of what is known to be possible by searching for solutions not yet conceivable. It encompasses integration of knowledge to be sure; but its goal is imaginative use of that integrated knowledge to find new and more effective solutions for old problems.

Not all professions organize their curriculums to help the student integrate knowledge. Law, engineering (except when on the cooperative basis), architecture, theology, and business administration do little, leaving most of the effort to the situation into which the graduate is projected for his first work in the profession. This

---

11 Charlotte Towle, *The Learner in Education for the Professions* (Chicago: The University of Chicago Press, 1954).

procedure leaves the integration of knowledge for use in practice to chance, and transfers responsibility from the school to the agency for a crucial part of professional education. It seems incredible that a profession will urge the establishment and expansion of professional schools, but will leave the final integration of the skill and knowledge which those schools help students to acquire to groups who are less capable of directing an educational experience than the schools themselves. Medicine has overcome the difficulty to some extent through directing the teaching hospital; dentistry through operating the dental clinic; teaching through the demonstration school; and social work through the designation of field supervisors for students placed in social work agencies. The lines of control in these illustrations run from the professional school to the agency, and modify the method so that the agency becomes an effective instrument of teaching students. Without this concern, teaching of application skills will always suffer.

Principles of curriculum organization. The organization of the curriculum is of profound significance for the professional school. Organization of the curriculum affects the difficulty with which the student masters its content, and the usefulness which that content will have for him. From the analyses which have appeared thus far, some principles can be drawn.

1. The curriculum should be organized in such a way that it moves from elementary to advanced subject matter, that it interests the student by exposing him quickly to the practice of his intended profession, and that it aids him to integrate its various parts into procedures which are useful in solving problems assigned to the profession. Since some of these ends are necessarily in opposition, organization of the curriculum is always a compromise among incompatibles.

2. The curriculum should be so organized that some experience with the practice of the profession appears early in the course, but it must also make sure that the student masters prerequisites before attempting advanced work.

3. The curriculum should be so organized that closely related courses parallel each other, with each contributing to the understanding of the other.

4. A student in the professional curriculum must integrate the knowledge and skills which he has acquired into a body of effective procedures in solving problems assigned to the profession. The professional school is responsible for assisting him in this task through all means at its disposal.

5. Integration is attained through use of knowledge and skill to solve problems for which the student is responsible. The clinical experience in the curriculum is of tremendous importance, therefore, in helping the student to integrate his learnings and to function as a professional person. Programs of internship or apprenticeship which are directed by the professional school have the great advantage of receiving guidance from persons who are more interested in education than they are in service alone. A profession which leaves field experience entirely to the control of the agencies of the profession is receiving less than those which ask their professional schools to direct this work.

6. No organization of the curriculum is wholly satisfactory. Experimentation is desirable to find the organization which best suits the objectives of the program.

CHAPTER V

The Problem of Instruction

The process by which a professional school helps a student to acquire the knowledge, skills, and attitudes he needs to practice his profession is known as *instruction*. As a term, *instruction* carries the unfortunate implication that learning in the student is derived solely from the teaching of the instructor, the instructor giving or presenting, the student receiving and absorbing.

Changes which occur in students cannot be based merely on transmission of information from the instructor's notes to the student's notebook. Instead, *instruction* is defined as a process of interaction in which the instructor, the student, other students, practitioners, books, laboratories, and other facilities all play essential parts. Since instruction is an interaction, its quality can be limited or improved by changing the quality of its parts. It is necessary to review each of these parts, for their quality determines the quality of instruction and therefore the quality of the graduate. And, ultimately, the quality of the graduates determines the quality of the profession.

The Faculty

Alfred North Whitehead, mathematician and philosopher, in writing about the aims of education, called for a faculty "whose learning is lighted up with imagination."[1] In so doing, he defined in part the kind of faculty member the professional schools search for constantly. No school wants a drudge, who drones through stale notes unconcerned with the significance or the freshness of his thought. Fortunately, this kind of instructor is diminishing as the demands for teachers of imagination increase. And the professional school is part of the change. As its teaching staff changed from practitioners to full-time faculty members, it also moved from de-

---

[1] Alfred North Whitehead, *The Aims of Education* (New York: The New American Library, 1956), p. 101.

55

pendence on persons for whom teaching was at best a sideline to persons for whom teaching was a way of existence. The part-time faculty member was a practitioner first and a teacher next. The full-time faculty member devotes his life and talents to the school of which he is a part, and gives the school the first call on his competence and energy. The shift was very important and very great. It made the professional school comparable to other divisions of the university.

It is difficult to realize how recently the change took place. Only twenty years ago, many medical schools had no full-time clinical faculty members. Planning the curriculum, careful study and appraisal of teaching methods, meticulous choice of students—none of these tasks could be done effectively with a part-time staff. Only as the professional school moved into the university was it able to provide more than proprietary schools had been able to offer. With the change came an atmosphere in which teaching and research could flourish as significant ends in themselves. A professor did not need to gain his reputation from practice. He could gain it from the excellence of his teaching and the significance of his research.

To recognize the importance of the full-time faculty member is not to ignore the usefulness of practitioners who serve as part-time teachers. Medical schools would be lost without them, for they often provide the only means of clinical teaching in many subspecialties, like neurosurgery or urology. Teacher education frequently depends on administrators and supervisors of the local school system. Social work calls upon practicing psychiatrists, physicians, and psychologists to discuss their special understanding of human beings. But it is the full-time faculty member whose contribution has become dominant.

One area of regression must be noted. Medical schools for years depended upon the part-time teacher for clinical courses. Full-time status released these teachers from the need for earning parts of their income by practice. As teachers, they treated the patients of the university hospital to instruct their students, not as sources of income. Nevertheless, clinical professors were constantly aware of the money that could be gained from practice and used the threat of entering private practice as a means of pressing their salaries to higher levels than those of any faculty in the medical school or in the university.

As salaries rose, the struggles of the university to pay them grew. To reduce the burden on the university, the device (almost the euphemism) of *geographic full-time* status was adopted. This elusive term means that the professor is not full-time at all. Instead he divides his time between academic functions and private practice, receiving parts of his income from each. "Geographic" merely means that the faculty member conducts his practice either in the university teaching hospital or very close to the medical school so that, the rationalization runs, the professor is available full-time to the school. He is not at all; he has reverted to the days when practitioners were the teachers. The only change is that teachers, under geographic full-time arrangements, are practitioners. That difference should not mask the fact that geographic full-time is not full-time, anymore than it would be full-time for a professor of education to hold a part-time position with the local school system as a guidance counselor. Geographic full-time should be recognized as the reversion it is. Medicine has almost lost the struggle for its clinical professors. Other professions should avoid similar failure, if at all possible.

Qualities needed. The interaction which learning represents is initiated and guided by the teacher. His responsibility grows from his knowledge of the field and his experience in selecting what is significant for persons entering the profession to study and learn. He must determine in large measure the content of the curriculum and must choose the methods which help learning to take place. The role of the faculty member is to guide the learning of students in directions in which he is himself competent and which are essential to the profession, either in practice, teaching, or research. This includes professional competence, social understanding, ethical behavior, and scholarly concern. Faculty members must be chosen with these objectives in mind.

A faculty member in a professional school must demonstrate *mastery of the knowledge* in his field. Usually, he is expected to obtain the highest degree or certification available to him. Professional fields show remarkable differences in their ability to attract new faculty members with a high proportion of doctor's degrees. For example, engineering has increased the proportion of new faculty members with doctor's degrees from about 16 per cent to 29 per cent in ten years; the health sciences, omitting dentistry and medicine, have dropped from about 34 per cent to about 14 per cent, and law from about 32 per cent to 19 per cent. Education has remained static at about 36 per cent.[2]

Degrees are significant, but acquisition of knowledge cannot be a static achievement. The faculty member must add to his knowledge as new facts and concepts become available. He must be a student throughout his life. He reflects and demonstrates, therefore, the need for continued study. He should be an example to his students, who will also be expected to continue to study throughout their lifetimes.

Knowledge underlies the significance of the teacher, and that knowledge should be as fresh and vibrant as the faculty member's own sense of constant discovery can make it. Particularly in a professional school, knowledge has the ultimate significance of solving problems of concern to human beings. It cannot be inert. The teacher's role is to be so aware of the excitement of learning that he cannot avoid transmitting that enthusiasm to his students. They are studying with him because of their interest and concern with the field he is teaching. Their interest is present. It needs only to be captured for the subject matter he commands.

This leads to the second desirable characteristic of the teacher— *desire and competence to teach.* A faculty member who looks upon teaching as an interruption to more important tasks can hardly be expected to transmit his knowledge or to guide students successfully in acquiring theirs. A faculty member who reluctantly teaches often expresses his frustrations through sarcasm and other verbal sadism to show his contempt for the whole process. His attitude destroys the possibility of effective interaction.

Desire to teach, important as it is, does not always equate with competence to teach. Apart from the obvious concerns of clarity of language, logic of presentation, willingness to be challenged, and skill in leading discussion, competence to teach is sometimes considered either so simple that there is nothing to learn, or so complex that nothing can be learned.

The fact is that students with innate capacity to teach still have many things to learn. Teaching is not composed of precise laws and

2 *Teacher Supply and Demand in Universities, Colleges, and Junior Colleges, 1961–62 and 1962–63* (Washington, D.C.: National Education Association, 1963), Table 3, p. 15.

sharply defined processes, but some methods of teaching are more successful than others. Gilbert Highet, a teacher of the classics, and author of *The Art of Teaching*,[3] emphasizes that teaching is not a "science," hence his title. The longest chapter of his book, however, is concerned with the teacher's methods, and other methods could be added to the ones he describes.

Competence to teach is a result of desire and of skill. Those who claim that knowledge is everything and method unimportant have not taken courses with some teachers whose knowledge is immense but whose teaching never reaches them.

A third characteristic of the effective teacher in the professional school is that of *belief in the significance of what he is doing*. Since a professional school has a steady focus on needs of the profession, the teacher must be convinced of the significance of that profession, or his service to it will be halfhearted. The field that he works in must, of course, capture his attention, but that is not enough. If he is a psychologist in a medical school, for example, he must be convinced that the medical profession is significant to society and teach psychology in relation to medical knowledge. If he is interested in psychology alone, he should transfer to the college of arts and sciences where psychology as a discipline appears in purer form.

Many other characteristics are significant in the teacher, but the final one to be given here is essential—*the continuing effort to learn*. A teacher never ceases learning. He is constantly revising his concepts and attitudes to make them fit more precisely with knowledge of the world. He will be active either in areas that interpret and assimilate new knowledge, or he will be active in research himself. If his teaching is concerned with the clinical or practical phases of the profession, he will faithfully try to increase his skills so that he can transmit them to his students. He will be experimental, so that he will not be limited to the known and accepted. And his desire to learn will keep him searching for the improved theory, skill, or concept which he can make available to students. His greatest satisfaction will come from the success of students who effectively serve their society through the profession for which he has taught, and he will be happiest when some of those students, stimulated by his

---

[3] Gilbert Highet, *The Art of Teaching* (New York: Vintage Books, 1958).

teaching, will advance in knowledge and skill beyond the point where he stands to become new leaders of the profession.

Recruitment and selection.   It is one thing to define the qualities needed in a faculty member for professional schools. It is quite another thing to find and acquire one with such qualities. Shortages in the professions affect faculties of professional schools even more sharply than they do the professions themselves, for shortages in the professions draw faculty members away from the schools and at the same time demand that the schools produce more graduates—which can only be done through obtaining more faculty members. The impact of these forces has created severe gaps in the faculties of professional schools throughout the country.

Most professional schools look for faculty members in other professional schools. Professional meetings have become hunting grounds for faculty members, sometimes in organized fashion. And it is a disappointing book which, upon publication, does not bring in its trail three or four offers of new positions to its author.

In professional fields where clinical or field instruction is especially important, schools sometimes recruit members of the practicing profession. This course is a gamble, because the practitioner usually has not ascended the academic ladder, learning his teaching tasks as he climbs. But sometimes the gamble pays handsomely, and the professional person is a remarkable teacher, stimulated by the interaction with other learning minds.

Recently, professional schools have begun to employ teachers and armed service personnel who have reached a required retirement age with abilities and energies unimpaired. Their experience and wisdom, together with their knowledge of their subjects, have placed some of them in great demand. To locate persons of this description a "retired professors registry" has been established. It distributes lists of available persons to universities and colleges.[4]

Professional schools will need to adopt other ways of recruiting as the shortages become more severe. Some professional schools are selecting promising graduates of their own, placing them on the faculty as instructors, and then assisting them to study for advanced degrees at other institutions on promise of return. Although expensive, this plan can fill vacancies that otherwise would not attract per-

---

[4] For information write to The Retired Professors Registry, 1785 Massachusetts Ave., Washington, D.C.

sons in other positions. The demand for college teachers with advanced degrees is bound to rise, at the same time that the number available to any one school will be declining.

Several kinds of scholarships are intended to increase the supply of college teachers. The Woodrow Wilson Fellowships are offered for the first year of graduate work. The National Science Foundation, the Atomic Energy Commission, and the National Institutes of Health offer support in their fields to advanced students. All these plans help to increase the supply of college teachers, but it is unlikely that the supply will match the demand as professional schools and professional students increase in numbers. Active efforts to recruit new faculty members will have to continue unabated.

Recruitment encourages desirable professional people to become interested in serving as faculty members of the professional schools. The choice of persons to be appointed to the faculty positions follows that step.

Selection of faculty members for professional schools varies little from selection for other divisions of universities. Usually there is no evidence of ability to teach, except through reputation on a campus reported by colleagues. Academic tradition excludes observers from the classroom, where evidence on competence in teaching could be sought. Knowledge of the field and continuing effort to learn are usually judged by degrees obtained and articles and books published. If the candidate has a substantial number of publications in his field, the conclusion is that he is continuing to learn, and that his knowledge of the field is satisfactory. If he is a senior faculty member at another institution, his record of academic advancement is evidence of competence. If he is fairly young, he will not have had time to publish or advance, and then the judgment must be based upon an assessment of his work in college and the opinions of teachers and colleagues. None of this evidence is wholly satisfactory.

Few schools use tests in selecting faculty, but many require personal interviews. The higher the rank the more likely personal interviews will be required. Some schools ask the candidate to conduct a seminar for faculty members on some subject related to his interest.

In general, the selection of faculty members for professional schools is a fairly haphazard procedure, because it has not been sufficiently studied to find satisfactory methods. The old method of selecting the practitioner with the largest reputation in town is no longer valid, but no better test has been advanced.

Income and benefits.   To some degree, the faculty member of a professional school is self-selected. He becomes a faculty member of a certain school because the functions of that position appeal to his desires and satisfy some of his needs. He can usually choose, however, between working in a professional school and private practice. In clinical medicine, he will often have gained an M.D. degree, and completed internship and residency. He usually will be licensed to practice. Inevitably, he will compare his position and income with those of other members of the profession, usually to his disadvantage. The demand for highly trained persons increases every year, and the professor of physics, for example, who used to be known only to his students, now converses easily with presidents.

The attractiveness of the academic life, however, is sufficient to interest a goodly number of graduates. They see the pleasures of relative freedom to follow intellectual pursuits. They see the delights of teaching young men and women to acquire an understanding of a complex field. They see the satisfactions of pursuing the unknown, with the possibility of making a discovery that may greatly affect the way human beings live or die. They see the zest of constantly dealing with matters of great moment in teaching and research, and, increasingly, in consultation with industry and government. Best of all, they find in teaching and research the elements of those things they enjoy most—intellectual excitement and self-directed effort. Some of these attributes are present in other occupations, but they are rarely found together in as nearly pure a form as they are on the campuses of universities.

These advantages do not eliminate the irritations and annoyances. Faculty members complain of committee work, but they complain even more bitterly when they or representatives of their departments are excluded from committees which they consider important. Sometimes teaching loads are so great that research or scholarship is impossible, but this sort of faculty exploitation is declining. Poverty, too, is no longer the universal mark of the teacher, particularly in the professional schools. The average income of physicians is about $18,000 a year. At a medical school in an eastern state, the heads of clinical departments receive a maximum of $35,000, of which $24,000 is derived from university funds and the remainder from approved practice as part of the geographic full-time arrangement. The American Association of University Professors eliminates medical school salaries from its computations, since to include them would skew the other figures greatly.

Other fields have not fared as well as medicine.[5] But the gap between the salaries of the campus and the market place is closing, and a competent person can follow his interests in teaching or research and still live comfortably.

In fact, the professional school may do well to avoid equalling the salaries offered by other agencies. The school must make sure that its faculty members live in some comfort or they will seek that comfort elsewhere, but a faculty member who leaves the campus for a government or industrial office simply to increase a satisfactory salary probably does not belong on a campus. He can find greater satisfaction in a more restrictive and directed atmosphere.

Organization. Faculties of professional schools are normally organized under a dean or director, and have been given substantial autonomy in the conduct of their affairs. The schools, however, surrender some freedom of decision when they enter the universities. Their budgets are subject to approval by the president and the board of trustees, but the president and the board assume considerable responsibility in finding funds for operation of the professional schools. Nevertheless, each professional school struggles for as much autonomy as it can obtain.

Various degrees of autonomy are allowed. The schools of the older professions, such as medicine and law, usually have the greatest autonomy. Schools of the newer professions, like nursing and social work, may have less autonomy, and may, in fact, be organized as departments of other schools or colleges. At some institutions, nursing is a department of the school of medicine. Social work schools, because of their desire to participate closely in the life of the university, are often subdivisions of the graduate school of the university, and submit to the general requirements and regulations of that organization.

The greatest difficulty in organization has appeared in teacher

---

[5] In dentistry, for example, "The mean salary of all full-time dental teachers was $8,568, compared to the mean net income of $14,311 for all nonsalaried, practicing dentists in 1958." Byron S. Hollinshead, Director, *The Survey of Dentistry* (Washington, D.C.: The American Council on Education, 1961), p. 367.

education, whose professional school may be too isolated or too weak to coordinate teacher education within the university. The National Council on Accreditation of Teacher Education (NCATE) has disturbed many a university by its insistence that programs of teacher education be effectively coordinated throughout the university. It has found that some universities believe that internal organization is none of NCATE's business.

The organization of professional education into schools has difficulties as the controversies with NCATE indicate. NCATE has urged that universities establish institution-wide committees or councils on teacher education and assign these committees responsibility for coordinating programs of teacher education throughout the institution. The committees are expected to make certain that comparable standards are employed where desirable, and that the quality of all programs reaches a minimum level, much as the graduate school does for graduate programs throughout the academic departments.

Coordination of programs in the professional fields is needed for all professional schools, not just for teacher education. Since the professional curriculum, with its content ranging from the basic arts and sciences, to the professional sciences, to the arts of application, calls for participation from more parts of the university than the professional school alone, some effective way to deal with the policies and procedures involved is needed. A university-wide council on professional education is preferable to one on teacher education alone. It could discover ways of off-setting the centrifugal forces that push professional education away from the central concerns of the university, and could help both the university and the professional schools find relationships that satisfy the demands and needs of each. A council could reduce the isolation of the professional schools without seriously affecting their autonomy. The council should be charged with working toward *achieving* rather than *requiring* coordination. Its method would be informing and persuading, not commanding. If it found itself in severe opposition with a professional school, it would appeal to the president and board of trustees for decision.

Within the professional schools, faculty organization has many variations. Without exception, the school is headed by an administrative officer, with the title of dean or director. Various associate administrators may be appointed to assist the major administrator in aspects of his work, as, for example, with admissions and student affairs, budget and finance, research programs, clinical or field agencies, and so on. Beyond that point, professional schools, like colleges of arts and sciences, are usually organized into departments, defined by special subject matters or skills. A medical school will usually be organized into various sorts of departments—biochemistry, a field of knowledge; anesthesiology or radiology, a group of skills as well as knowledge; and preventive medicine, which is a set of approaches within which the knowledge and skills taught elsewhere in the school are focused and directed. A school of social work, on the other hand, may depend more greatly on the rest of the university for its prerequisite courses, and will be organized into departments that reflect 1) the methods used in social work practice, like casework, groupwork, and community organization, and 2) the settings in which social work is practiced, like medical or psychiatric. A school of engineering may include departments of physics, mathematics, chemistry, or even English, but more often it depends on the arts and sciences college for these subjects and limits its departments to those dealing with the professional sciences clustered around major occupational divisions like civil engineering, mechanical engineering, electrical engineering, and chemical engineering.

Although the department is the most common form of organization, the system has its difficulties, since problems of a profession do not neatly correspond to departmental organization. Where this is recognized, institutes are established to assemble from the departments those faculty members who have a common interest. A research institute, for example, may assist members from various departments to execute research contracts. It is true that the projects which the institute undertakes require competencies which are located in the various departments, but an institute is needed to penetrate the departmental lines. A family life institute, for another example, may call upon faculty members from the law school, the medical school, and the school of social work, as well as the schools of home economics and public health. The institute serves to supplement the departments without supplanting them.

Coordination may sometimes be achieved by organizing a council composed of representatives of the different departments and by using that body to reach conclusions on policy. This device has the advantage of leaving the departments intact, but of overcoming some of their difficulties. Dual appointments to more than one department, or even more than one school, can improve coordination as well as help a faculty member use his capacities to the fullest.

Integration of the professional schools, particularly in the health fields, has been met in some universities by establishing positions of vice-president or vice-chancellor whose duties include coordination of the schools dealing with health—medicine, dentistry, nursing, pharmacy, and public health. These fields have developed so many relationships with the community and state and federal governments that they cannot be permitted to function alone, for each has significance for the others. Furthermore, some functions can be combined, saving the need for dual buildings or personnel. About twenty-five universities now have vice-presidents for health affairs, often the dean of the medical school, who is given the additional function and title, but sometimes a person separate from any of the deans. The University of Pittsburgh has gone even further. It has both a vice-chancellor for health affairs and a vice-president for the professions. The latter has responsibility for all professional schools other than those dealing with health.

Principles to follow. The principles to follow in selecting and maintaining a faculty of a professional school are not greatly different from those which are to be followed for any faculty. The faculty of a professional school must be able to serve its purpose of preparing its graduates to enter a profession, and be adept in developing its relationships on the one side with the arts and sciences college and on the other with the practitioners. Some faculty members will have close relationships with the teachers of basic arts and sciences in the college; others will have closer relationships with the practicing profession. Both, however, have a primary responsibility to the professional school. These peculiarities suggest the following principles concerning faculty:

1. A faculty member in a professional school must demonstrate knowledge of his field, interest and competence in teaching, and conviction on the significance of the subject matter he teaches and the profession he serves. He must continue to learn, either through scholarship which consolidates and interprets new knowledge as it appears, or through active research which adds to knowledge.

2. The university, because of continuing shortages of faculty members

for its professional schools, must constantly encourage potential teachers to consider joining its faculty.

3. Selection of faculty members for professional schools is a fairly haphazard process. A university should select faculty members on what bases it can use, such as reputation as a teacher, publication record, opinions of colleagues, academic record, and personal interviews. Careful studies isolating the factors of selection and testing the results against later success might be useful.

4. The university must be able to provide its faculty members with sufficient income to supply a comfortable living, but it should not attempt to match salaries available in other situations. Unless the intellectual life of a university is attractive in and of itself, the faculty member will not be successful.

5. The university should maintain full-time positions in its professional schools. In full-time positions, the teacher's functions are limited to teaching and research. Practice is restricted to that amount which aids teaching and research. It is not undertaken in order to supplement salaries.

6. The university should increase the attractiveness of its positions by allowing all the freedom possible to its faculty members to pursue ends which interest them, particularly in research.

7. The university must coordinate the work of professional schools with the other functions of the university. It may have to establish special means of coordination, either through university-wide councils or vice-presidents. The autonomy of the professional school must be limited by the need of unified action.

8. The professional school will continue to be organized into departments, based on parts of knowledge or special functions. Increasingly, however, the professional school will find it necessary to supplement the departmental structure with institutes concerned with special areas that cut across the boundaries of departments.

Methods of Instruction

The interaction or instruction that takes place among a teacher, students, and a subject matter is affected by the method chosen for the purpose. The method will vary with the skill of the teacher and the interest of the students, but most of all the method must be appropriate to the purpose of instruction. If that purpose is to transmit information, one method will serve; if it is to develop skills, other methods must be employed; and if the hope is to combine knowledge and skill in the solution of professional problems, still other methods will serve best. Some methods can be used for a variety of purposes, but others are limited in their usefulness.

For transmitting or acquiring information.   In a great part of education, the professor transmits information to the student, and the dominant method of doing so is the lecture. It is amazing that the lecture has remained almost unchanged from the medieval university. Professors still speak from their notes, even though the library contains books with much the same information in them. Students take notes on the lectures and prepare for examinations by reviewing the notes. In fact, the lecture is a rapid device for transmitting or at least presenting information. Its fault is that it fails to establish interaction with students. When students complain more of boredom than of hard work, they are usually thinking of lectures.

There are mechanical variations of lectures such as films, tapes, and more recently, closed circuit television. These are novel and quickly capture the attention of students, but they require effective lecturers in order to be assured that interaction takes place.

The seminar is a significant change from the lecture. It is appropriate for advanced students, and is guided to some extent by their own interests. A member of the seminar will present a paper. The others will discuss the paper, analyzing its content and suggesting ways its ideas could be strengthened or improved. Seminars place students in the position of discussing topics with colleagues, using their professor as a person to whom appeals can be made and from whom general guidance may be expected. The instructor is not looked to as the fount of all wisdom, however. Students take the responsibility of finding much of the information for themselves.

These and other methods of presenting information are used by the professional school, particularly when it feels pressed for time and must give as much as it can as quickly as possible. The lecture, either given in person or by film or television, may be the only way a famed person can be brought before students. Where possible, a question period should follow the lecture to eliminate confusion and to consider points of particular interest to the students.

But use of the classroom merely to transmit information is wasteful if that information is available to the students on their own time. The library is an integral part of the professional school, particularly as the profession depends more and more upon the sciences. A curriculum that requires students to spend so much time in the classroom that they have none left for the library is poorly designed. After graduation, the student will have to depend heavily on books and articles for information he needs. He should begin to develop this kind of dependence in his student days.

The laboratory, especially in the sciences, serves as a method for acquiring information and developing skills. To a scientist, a course without a laboratory is hardly worth the time it takes, since students merely hear about science rather than participate in scientific procedures. In the laboratory, the student recreates some of the experiments that advanced knowledge in times past, works through a number of skills required by laboratory research, and eventually may make his own discoveries. The use of the laboratory has been extended beyond the physical sciences to include any grouping of materials that can be used to produce new results, such as *curriculum laboratory* or *reading laboratory*, in which students use a variety of materials in preparing outlines of curriculums or methods and materials for teaching reading.

For developing skills. The curriculums of the professional schools are usually organized so that a student progresses from knowledge to skills. Sometimes these areas of learning are parallel so that the students acquire the skills while they gain the knowledge of the profession. To teach skills, the instructor often follows the sequence of presentation, demonstration, execution, and evaluation. He first describes the elements of the skill and demonstrates it. Then he asks the student to execute the procedure, first with close supervision and slow performance, then with increasing speed through repetition, and finally with no supervision but a later check to see how closely the performance matches standards. Some skills can be learned quickly and measured precisely, such as a means of recording data; but others are difficult to master and impossible to evaluate definitively, such as lecturing or interviewing. Even for these more complicated skills, however, the student can learn from an instructor and improve under his supervision.

The professional school is more concerned with the development of skills than the arts and sciences college, for skills buttressed with knowledge contain the substance of practice. A surgeon must be able to use a scalpel, a civil engineer a transit, a dentist the drill, and a social worker the interview, regardless of his other knowledge or skill. The skills these instruments require are essential parts of professional competence.

Teaching skills requires smaller groups of students than transmitting knowledge through the lecture. In this fact lies one reason why the professional school is expensive. The process of teaching skills can be aided by films, slides, and television, but none of these can supplant the instructor who painstakingly demonstrates a skill and then supervises the student as he acquires it.

For establishing attitudes. Knowledge, skills, and attitudes are the time-worn goals of education. They are equally goals of professional education, and the third, attitudes, requires its own methods. A professional school hopes to aid its students to adopt attitudes which are appropriate to that calling. Each profession has its set of values, and it earnestly desires that its new members will be guided by them. It establishes a code of ethics to help its members understand their obligations. To some observers, the ethical component more than any other characteristic distinguishes a profession from other ways of making a living.

Since ethical behavior is of such surpassing importance to the professions, it should be easy to isolate methods of developing attitudes. Unfortunately, it is not, because the professional schools are doing too little and are confused about what should be done. No more than half the schools of social work and medicine or two-thirds of the schools of law, allocate any time at all in their curriculums to the subject of professional ethics. Some dispose of the subject in a lecture or two. Others call on local practitioners to explain the intricacies of practice, which may turn out to be explanations on how to collect bills and keep appointments. One school tells of posting the code in the entrance hall to make sure that every student sees it!

Much more could be done. A faculty member or a preceptor can point out the many choices a professional person must make in executing his tasks. Teachers can review a student's work to assess both its accuracy and the attitudes it reflects. Schools can experiment with the use of case studies to illustrate problems of professional ethics, and they can use socio-dramas to demonstrate a problem and present it in human terms for class discussion. They can use the stories of the daily press to illustrate points at which attitudes become significant. Schools have been successful in teaching the attitudes of objectivity and honesty which lie behind the scientific method. If they are wise, they will struggle to be as effective in inculcating other attitudes, particularly those which appear in the codes. No profession can long absorb the poison of unethical practice without courting death.

For the art of application. Professional schools use methods in transmitting information and in developing skills that are comparable to those used in the other parts of the university. The professional sciences are taught in much the same way as the basic sciences with lecture and laboratory as the main devices. Most professional schools, however, are not satisfied to end their concern with transmitting information or developing individual skills. They want to assist students in the art of application, or, to put it more explicitly, in the process of combining knowledge and skill in procedures that will solve or reduce problems in fields assigned to the profession.

The art of application is the art of practice, never wholly a science because the factors involved are too numerous to fit into formulae, and never wholly susceptible to manuals and recipes. A profession's major responsibilities always require judgment based on knowledge concerning the problems to be solved and the means by which solutions are possible.

Originally, professional education was part apprenticeship and part academic instruction. Apprenticeship became inadequate when knowledge began to revolutionize practice. Without knowledge, practice would be little more than guesswork. Apprenticeship was effective in teaching the art, but it could not keep pace with the expansion of knowledge. To do that, professors with time and opportunity for research and study were required to keep abreast of the new knowledge and to transmit it to students and to the profession. But they could not provide, by themselves, the art of application. Knowledge of that art had to come from practice, not from study, from acting, not from receiving.

It is this combination of academic study and apprenticeship learning which gives professional education its peculiar and significant character. Professional education is more unusual in its efforts to develop the art of application than it is in providing instruction in the professional sciences and skills.

Methods on the campus. As earlier discussion showed, schools in some professions do a great deal toward application prior to the student's graduation. These are presented in the form of *problems or cases* that the student must solve. They therefore require the integration of knowledge and skill. Schools of architecture, for example, both teach and test competence in design by assigning problems of increasing complexity. Problems are similar to the facts that the architect will have before him when he sits down to design a structure to fit a client's needs. It calls forth all the student has learned and requires him to relate the parts to the whole.

Engineering aids the student in the integration and synthesis of knowledge and skill by the *project method* in which, again, the student is presented with complex situations and asked to find the engineering solution, considering the materials available, the costs involved, and the requirements of the client.

The *case method* is another kind of simulated situation in which the student tries to find a solution for a set of facts. Law schools, beginning with Harvard in the 1870's, have used the case method almost to the exclusion of other methods of instruction. The records of cases taken to the appellate courts form the body of facts which the student analyzes, trying to draw from them principles of law that can be followed in other situations. By studying the cases, students learn what significant steps the opposing counsels took and what precedents controlled the court's decision. Most of all they find ways to correlate what they have learned from other cases with the case at hand. Since this process is precisely what they must do when they enter the courtroom after admission to practice, the case method is an excellent introduction to the requirements of practice. It allows students to derive principles from actual legal situations and decisions instead of accepting principles without thought or analysis.

Other fields in the social sciences have found the case method useful. Business administration, again first at Harvard, introduced the use of case studies as a means of testing and integrating the knowledge which students had gained in classroom and library. Cases which are carefully wrought descriptions of facts relating to business decisions were collected over a period of years. In fact, Harvard found that it took eight years to change from the lecture system to the case method. Business schools do not have a convenient record such as court proceedings on which the law schools depend, and, like schools in other professions which use cases for study, had to collect cases from practice laboriously, and just as laboriously keep the cases up to date as new concepts and techniques were developed. But the usefulness of dealing with a concrete set of facts that had had significance in an industry offset the difficulties.

Public administration has collected a series of cases for study, but does not use them as widely as law or business. Social work schools use cases frequently, particularly in the intricacies of teaching casework. The Council on Social Work Education makes significant case studies available to the schools of social work after modifying the names and locations to avoid revealing confidences. The Council even distributes films and tape recordings which present cases for analysis and decision.

Research studies are another means of integrating the knowledge and skill which the student has obtained, particularly in those fields where careful preparation of data is a required part of practice. These include clinical psychology, which takes the research-oriented Doctor of Philosophy degree as its requirement for entrance into the profession; social work, which requires the master's degree, usually with a thesis; engineering, which often calls for a senior research paper of considerable scope; and several others. Some medical schools are beginning to require a research experience, either during the regular year or summer session.

The most important and complex of the methods for instruction in application is the *teaching clinic,* a term used here to encompass all the actual practice situations which occur before graduation and which involve services to a clientele outside the school. The term includes the clinics and wards of the teaching hospital, the dental clinic, the psychological clinic, the veterinary medical clinic, and the demonstration school. The teaching clinic is partially designed to help the student learn skills, but its main purpose is to help him combine knowledge and skills in solving problems, in other words, in application. The student's work is executed under supervision to make certain that his mistakes are corrected, and their dangers to the client are minimized. His work is organized for the purpose of his learning, not for the purpose of serving the client, although the two coincide in ideal moments.

Medicine, dentistry, and veterinary medicine devote most of their second two years to study in the teaching clinic. In medicine, the student first learns how to take case histories, those records of the patient's life and medical history which help form the basis of diagnosis. Under supervision, the student learns how to meet and examine a patient, to make laboratory tests where necessary, and to propose a tentative diagnosis. This diagnosis, from which treatment will be determined, is discussed with instructors and other students. At the beginning, however, the student has no responsibility for treatment.

Beyond this initial phase, students enter clinical clerkships in which they become part of the medical team, not only obtaining the initial history but continuing with the patient after treatment and reporting medical progress to the team. The student learns to search for new solutions when the progress of the case does not follow expectations. He moves from specialty to specialty after fairly brief periods of time. A student's progress in the teaching clinics is frequently checked. His most rigorous test comes in the clinico-pathological conferences. In these the student is given the case history of a patient who has died, and is asked to make a diagnosis of the illness. His diagnosis is checked against the postmortem findings. An inadequate diagnosis quickly becomes apparent.

Dental schools, like medical schools, use much of the last two years for work in the clinic, which is operated by the dental school itself. The student learns to execute increasingly difficult dental procedures, starting with the repair of simple caries and ending with dental surgery. Members of the faculty carefully supervise the student and check his work before the patient is released. The patients come from the community and are usually unable to pay the full costs of dental service.

Some schools are conducting experimental programs in the dental clinics under which the students learn to work with dental assistants in performing their tasks. The dental students call upon the assistants to aid them in furthering the work, learning in the process how to use dental assistants effectively. Since the American Dental Association has estimated that a dentist can double the number of patients he treats by using dental assistants and hygienists effectively, it is important for dental students to learn how to use these auxiliary persons. Doing so can help reduce the continuing shortage of dentists without increasing the number of dentists at all.

The veterinary clinic is run in much the same way as the dental clinic. To it are brought patients in need of the clinic's services, and in it students learn how to practice in the field they have chosen. Most of the last two years of veterinary medical school are devoted to work in the clinic, dealing first with small animals and then with large animals. The student makes diagnoses, orders treatment, and follows the patients into recovery. Veterinary medical schools have elaborate equipment and large buildings to make the clinic work possible. They will spend considerable sums trucking animals to the clinic if needed to provide sufficient amounts of "clinical material" for the students to work with. As in medicine and dentistry, the students work under the supervision of the faculty, executing increasingly difficult procedures after they demonstrate their competence in the simpler phases of their profession's work.

Campus psychological clinics also deal with clients from the community. When fully used for teaching, they often use one-way glass so that students can follow interviews being conducted by faculty members, and interviews conducted by students can be followed and later discussed by faculty members. In one variation, closed circuit TV cameras are focused through the one-way glass and the screen placed before a group of students. In the psychological clinics, like the others, students progress from simple to more complex procedures, and from very close supervision to greater freedom.

In the sense in which the term is used in this chapter, a campus *demonstration school* is a teaching clinic. The demonstration school was once considered such an essential part of teacher education that many a campus was graced with an elementary and secondary school operated by the university itself. In the school, students undertook their practice teaching under observation and guidance of faculty members who formed the staff of the school in much the same way that medical faculty members form the staff of the university hospital. The concept on which this elaborate structure was raised was simple: to teach students to teach well, the university must control the teaching clinic, the school. It can do this only if it actually conducts the school. Hence the demonstration school.

The demonstration school had disadvantages. It was costly. It was abnormal, since its pupils came largely from faculty families. It did little to help the students learn the kind of situations they would have to contend with when they graduated. As a result, universities have tended to give up the demonstration school, or at the very least, to supplement it with experiences in the neighboring schools.[6] Universities find that use of neighboring schools avoids some of the difficulties even though it presents others. Selecting the school and the teachers is complicated, for example, by the fact that the teaching may not be of a quality that students should adopt. Some colleges have provided supplements to teachers' salaries, both to repay them for the extra work they do in supervising students and to allow the school board to recruit more competent teachers. Others have found it essential to conduct summer workshops or seminars throughout the regular sessions for the teachers they expect to use in supervising students. The school of education cannot afford to be content merely with what is available in the schools if the quality of teaching is low.

Methods off the campus.   A profession usually finds that it cannot complete all the work in application which it wishes to accomplish by staying on the campus, even when that campus is equipped with teaching hospital or demonstration school. Instead, the agencies of the profession aid the school in shaping the student to enter the profession, and some continue this under organized programs even after the student begins his practice.

The best known of these methods is *internship,* a term which in this country is primarily used to describe the first year of wholly practical training which a medical student receives in a hospital after he obtains his degree. When dentistry, veterinary medicine, teaching, or even law talks about the need for establishing internships, it is thinking of this pattern. Universally, medical graduates who expect to practice enter internships, and this internship forms the final organized, full-time training for the general practitioner in medicine. The internships are very popular with hospitals which depend on the interns and the resident physicians to provide "house coverage," that is, to be available at all times that a physician may be required, even though a patient's own doctor is not present. Pay is often low and the work arduous, but for a medical graduate it is the crucial period when he is recognized for the first time as a colleague by other physicians.

Internships are tending to become "straight" internships. In these, the graduate spends all his time on one sort of service, medical, sur-

---

6 See G. K. Hodenfield and T. M. Stinnett, *The Education of Teachers* (Englewood Cliffs, N.J.: Prentice-Hall, Inc., 1961), p. 86; Spectrum, S 17.

gical, pediatric, or other. The older internship was "rotating," in which the intern moved from specialty to specialty at set intervals, being exposed to the major clinical fields within the year's period. Half the year was divided between internal medicine and surgery; the other half among pediatrics, obstetrics, public health, psychiatry or other clinical specialty. But, according to accrediting regulations, no less than two months can be spent on any one service; no more than three specialties can be added in the second six months.

The purpose of the rotating internship is to give the graduate experience in most of the areas he will meet after he enters practice on his own. The rotating internship qualifies him for general practice; the straight internship leads him toward becoming a medical specialist. General practitioners, therefore, support the rotating internships; medical specialists uphold the straight internships.

The quality of internships varies greatly from one hospital to another. Some hospitals attract interns with little effort; others rarely fill their posts. The difference in attractiveness lies more in the quality of training than in any other one factor, even the salaries which the internships earn. Salaries are small in the most attractive internships, larger in the less attractive. Interns want to serve where there are indigent patients so that they can have responsibility for patient care, but they also want the teaching accompanying these cases to be of good quality, guided if possible by an adequate staff and planned by faculty members or directors of medical education.[7] Hospitals or medical schools which cannot meet these requirements have difficulty in attracting sufficient numbers of interns, because about 12,000 internships compete for 7,000 medical graduates each year. A portion of the gap is filled with graduates of foreign medical schools, but the competition for graduates of domestic schools is so keen that the salaries paid are beginning to rise to almost a living wage.

When dentistry is concerned with developing specialists, it establishes internships. In dental surgery, for example, internships are established at hospitals under the guidance of the dental school. They have much the form of the straight medical internship.

Architecture uses what it calls a *Candidate Training Program*

---

[7] See Ralph E. Dolkart, *et al.*, "Hospitals which Do and Do Not Fill Their Intern Quotas," *Journal of Medical Education*, Vol. 33, No. 10 (October, 1958), 721–725.

which has many similarities to the medical internship. The graduate in architecture obtains a position with an architectural firm, but he works as "architect-in-training" even though an employee of the firm. He is considered a student during the three years of his internship, and is expected to learn how to apply his knowledge to problems which the office is required to meet, with increasing responsibility for success of the design. The architect who employs the graduate serves as his preceptor throughout this period, but the graduate may also meet in seminars with graduates in other firms. He is expected to keep a log-book in which to record his experiences and learnings day by day. Sometimes other architects advise him on his progress.

Clinical psychology uses an internship within the third year of the usual program leading to the Ph.D. degree. The internship, like that of medicine, is conducted in an agency not under the control of the faculty, and the usual conflicts develop between the purposes of education and the purposes of performing the agency's work. Faculty members select the agencies in which internships can be accepted and provide some supervision of the programs as they proceed. But too often there is little contact between the faculties and the agencies, and the student is left largely to his own abilities during that year to obtain the experience he needs. It is an unusually important year, because the student is expected to use the internship period to begin research on the dissertation which he will complete during the fourth year of graduate education after he returns to the campus.

Student teaching is comparable to the internship of medicine, except that it is undertaken prior to graduation. The school of education exercises considerable responsibility in making sure that the students obtain as full an educational experience as possible. Social work goes even further. It parallels its academic work with *field instruction,* or experience in agency work, so that classes and agency instruction run concurrently. When distances to adequate social work agencies are too great for this sort of organization, social work schools send the students away for "blocks" of time, in which they work full-time within the agencies. The concurrent arrangement is preferred because under it the faculty can aid the students to grasp the relationships between the theoretical formulations of the classrooms and the realities of the agencies.

Medicine and clinical psychology use another form of experience, called in medicine a *preceptorship* and in psychology a *clerkship*. In these the student works closely with a practitioner, learning from him. This is similar to the older apprenticeship program from which the apprentice emerged from indenture to become a journeyman. Medicine has reduced its use of the preceptorship, partly because it now uses summers more frequently for research programs for students, and partly because it saw inescapable weaknesses in the almost totally unsupervised preceptorships. Psychology has continued to use the clerkship as an introduction to practice, but depends much more on the later internship to raise students to the level of beginning practice.

The *residencies* which medicine has established in all the special fields are now so well accepted that they can hardly be shaken. They are outside the jurisdiction of the medical schools except that many are conducted within teaching hospitals of the schools. In general, the residencies are continuations of the straight internships. A young physician who has completed his internship obtains a residency in a speciality he wishes to enter, and may stay within that residency for as long as five years. He will be paid much less than he could earn as a general practitioner, for which he is already qualified, but his intent is to become a specialist, and the rank of specialist is attained only through a residency. He will be assigned increasingly responsible duties, and he will supervise and teach interns while he is a resident. Both experiences will be useful to him as he strives toward his goal of becoming a specialist.

Principles of instruction. The great variety of methods which professional education employs is required by the variety of its goals. It cannot be content with merely purveying information no matter how important. It must help a student learn to use knowledge in the solution of significant problems, and it must help him learn how to continue to grow in wisdom and skill throughout his professional lifetime. In choosing methods to use, the professional educator can find certain principles to guide him. These he must test against his own abilities and experience so that he uses those which are most effective. He must constantly evaluate success, however, by the effectiveness with which students learn to apply knowledge in practice or acquire new knowledge through research. The principles he should test are similar to the following.

1. Instructional methods should be consciously chosen. The teacher should not merely repeat the methods which he observed as a student.

2. Methods should be chosen in accordance with the objective sought, the students to be affected, and the instructor who uses them. Methods which are effective and economical in transmitting information may be ineffective in modifying attitudes.

3. Methods used should be subject to evaluation, and should be changed when it becomes apparent that other methods would be more effective or more economical in guiding learning.

4. Methods used should encourage "active" rather than "passive" attitudes in students wherever possible, so that students will develop the self-reliant scholarship which can carry them throughout their careers.

5. Methods used to instruct in application must be carefully designed and supervised for their educational effects to avoid such emphasis on "service" or "production" that the educational aspect of the experience for the student is subordinated to need of the agency to get the job done.[8]

6. Work-experience programs, if well planned and managed, can be of great benefit to students both in learning the art of application and in helping them to integrate knowledge and skill obtained through other methods.

7. Careful organization and supervision can so increase the efficiency of work-experience programs that the time devoted to them can be reduced without loss of learning or danger to the client.

8. New methods, such as programmed instruction or closed circuit television, should be used experimentally to determine their effectiveness. They should neither be discarded because new or adopted because others have found them helpful.

9. If two methods are equally effective, the more economical should be chosen.

10. The choice of method must ultimately be left to each instructor, since within the limits of cost he must choose those methods with which he is most experienced. The school has an obligation, however, to aid instructors to become aware of the variety of methods that may be employed so that they can choose those which are effective for them and

---

[8] Herbert A. Thelen has suggested the term "reflective action" to connote "action carried out in an educative manner. For action to be reflective action it must engage the conscious mind; it must have an active intellectual component; it must involve purposive goal-seeking, diagnosis, creating hypotheses, rehearsing action in one's mind, connecting causes to effects, finding commitments, seeing relationships between each step and long-range aims, and so on. And these processes must be seen together as comprising a strategy of action." (These attributes are precisely what the professional educator hopes will come from the internship or other work-experience, but he is wise enough to know that work-experience is not always conducted with such precision of purpose.) See Herbert A. Thelen, *Education and the Human Quest* (New York: Harper & Row, Publishers, 1960), p. 172ff.

for students. At some point, therefore, an analysis and evaluation of teaching is needed, either by colleagues, curriculum committee, or supervisor.[9]

---

[9] The Association of American Medical Colleges has been conducting annual seminars on teaching for a number of years. Also, the work of George Miller and others at the University of Illinois has sharpened the focus of medical educators on methodology as a proper subject of study and experimentation. See George Miller, ed. *Teaching and Learning in Medical School* (Cambridge, Mass.: Harvard University Press, 1961). Another useful volume is Charlotte Towle, *The Learner in the Professions* (Chicago: The University of Chicago Press, 1954). Dr. Towle is particularly penetrating in discussing the effects of the internship, or field instruction, on the student.

CHAPTER VI

The Problem of Students

A student is both the raw material and the product of the professional school. Educators in the United States have concluded that research and teaching should go hand in hand, each aiding the other. The isolated research institute appears infrequently, since the university with its concern for both research and teaching is the more customary pattern of organization. Even the Rockefeller Institute, established on the Germanic model of the separated research institute, has begun to award advanced degrees in its fields of competence.

A professional school has an inescapable obligation to teach. Because it has become almost the exclusive channel for entrance into its field, its students will determine the quality of the profession. Continuing shortages of qualified students will inevitably reduce the quality of the profession itself and will encourage clients to find other ways of obtaining the assistance they seek. The work of the school supports the profession it serves. It must obtain enough students and it must obtain good enough students or the profession suffers.

The need for sufficient numbers of students is clearly seen, but defining the qualities which students must have if they are to become effective members of the profession is more complicated.

Definition of Qualities Desired

No one knows precisely what qualities of students will best serve the professional fields. As professional men, the graduates will be required to be both scholars and practitioners, even though the two roles are sometimes in conflict. In their pure form, the roles appear opposite. The scholar is essentially an onlooker, an analyzer, a recorder, who holds aloof from the functions he studies in order that his results will not be warped by his emotional reactions to the facts or to their implications. His highest value as a scholar will be objectivity which he can achieve only by avoiding involvement and commitment. The folk knowledge places him in an "ivory tower," and considers him an "egghead," without warmth or sympathy, useful, perhaps, but not liked.

On the other hand, the practitioner whether doctor, nurse, teacher, or lawyer can function effectively only if he elicits the faith and trust of his client. He will expect the client to do a number of things which may be dangerous, unpleasant, or bothersome, and he cannot hope that the client will follow his directions unless he inspires trust. Society protects the practitioner in this relationship by allowing information supplied him by his client "privileged" status, meaning the practitioner need not divulge confidences of his client. The folk knowledge considers the doctor as a man at the bedside of the ill and feeble, the nurse as a cool hand on a fevered brow, the teacher as happiest when surpassed by his gifted pupil, willing to spend long hours outside of school to help the dullard keep pace, and the lawyer as the friend as well as the confidant of criminal and saint alike. These pictures are romanticized, but they represent deep-seated attitudes of society towards those in whom it has faith.

The two roles conflict. No one can be objective and subjective simultaneously; no one can be withdrawn and outgoing at the same time. Luckily, the roles need not overlap in time, since the professional man can switch from one to another as needed. In fact, he cannot afford to remain either one or the other. If he is entirely the student, he cannot make effective contact with clients; if he is wholly the practitioner, he cannot bring to his clients the knowledge which is added daily to his profession.

Students for the professional schools must be selected to be both scholars and practitioners, with characteristics that are appropriate to both future roles. Even with this complication in mind, it is possible to identify some of the characteristics which students being admitted to professional school should display.

An active, inquiring intelligence of high order. The student in a professional school will need to absorb large masses of abstract material in order to gain the knowledge and skill which practice demands. That body of knowledge is the profession's most important attribute. Anyone entering the profession must master that knowledge. Furthermore, the student cannot merely absorb the information and knowledge. He must actively test new knowledge and work it through his own experience until it becomes his in use as well as in memory. His inquiring mind must search for better solutions than he has yet found and learn from all sources open to it—books, people, experience, and reflection.

All of this takes an intelligence of high order, even though the degree of intelligence may vary considerably from profession to profession and from individual to individual within a profession. Each profession searches for students of high intelligence. The ones it chooses must have above average intellectual ability. Otherwise, they cannot survive the professional school curriculums.

A stable personality. A professional person is called upon to aid others, and the demands upon him are often severe and lengthy. His clients will place their problems in his hands, and he will be unable to care for them if he himself is in severe conflict with his role or his ability to assist. Geniuses will be able to make great contributions in spite of instability, but these people are the exceptions. In selecting students for the professional school, educators look for stable persons who have resolved their own internal conflicts to a large extent, and who appear to have achieved sufficient integration to make their abilities effective.

A commitment to the field. A profession's demands cannot be met by a person to whom the field is merely a means of support. Long hours, strenuous effort, and a pervading sense of inadequacy are present in every profession. There are always more problems than solutions. A physician has to accept the fact that ultimately he will fail in preserving the health of every patient, and the teacher must recognize that the ideal he maintains of the fully developed scholar will be attained by few of his students. Without a strong commitment, the professional man cannot hope to withstand temptations of shoddy work or selfish gain. He can maintain the ethic of the profession only as it lives in his commitment.

Sufficient self-confidence to permit flexibility and experimentation. The student who enters professional school is embarking on the first few miles of a journey which may take thirty or forty years to complete. His career will be marked by many changes in situation and practice caused by social changes over which he will have little control and compelled by the additions of knowledge to his profession. If he is so ridden with fear and anxiety that he clings desperately to the familiar and finds comfort only in a rigidly regulated existence, he is hardly fit material for the profession.

Instead, students with sufficient confidence in themselves will find excitement in change and satisfaction in experiments directed toward finding better ways of doing familiar things even if new procedures must be adopted. No profession has completed its growth and no professional person can be effective if he holds tenaciously to the past. Students must bring into the school with them this willingness to welcome change.

Educators look for a number of other characteristics when selecting students for the professional schools, and the different professions put varying values on the ones suggested. Students entering the "helping" professions should be sensitive to people. Students entering fields like engineering and architecture need a passion for exactness, for much of what they do requires mathematical precision. Some professions, like medicine and dentistry, require a combination of both. Certainly all professions require physical energy. The sickly genius will not fit the standard, but, again, may be the exception. The prospective student should be a healthy person.

Recruitment and Selection

Professional schools recruit in various ways. For undergraduate programs like teaching and forestry, recruitment must take place in high schools where the students are making up their minds on college and careers. The student high school counselor is an important person in this process, for he advises students and guides other teachers. Much of the professional literature is directed toward him, and many professions send representatives to career days which the guidance counselor organizes.

Student clubs capture the attention of students who already have some interest in a professional field, and help to keep that interest alive with information about the field. Some agencies have employed high school students during the summers to work as aides or helpers to expose them to the satisfactions and the difficulties of work in the field. Pamphlets, lectures, motion pictures, and visits all are used to interest students in a field.

None of the professions believes that enough is being done for the shortages continue to exist. As a result, the most potent forms of recruiting—scholarships, fellowships, and loans—have expanded until it takes a four volume work to describe them all.[1] Each year the federal government adds to these appropriations, and more university funds go into them. The hope is that ultimately every student who has the capacity and interest to enter a professional field will be able to do so, regardless of his financial position. A 1962 government report proposed that *all* graduate students in engineering, mathematics, and physical sciences receive adequate financial support.[2]

Recruiting students is a necessity, but it does no good to admit students who will not be able to finish the course. Schools must choose, from among those interested, the students who can become qualified entrants into the professions. When the school makes its selection, it enters another process in which complete success is impossible.

Schools first look to see whether the applicant has completed earlier studies. All professional schools now require prospective students to complete courses which are prerequisite to admission. They did not even a short while ago. In 1910, Abraham Flexner vigorously urged medical schools to establish admission standards by requiring at least graduation from high school and preferably completion of two years of college. Since then prerequisites have become universal, although the professions show little uniformity on what is required.

The professional fields exhibit the following patterns with regard to prerequisites needed for entry.

social work clinical psychology theology	bachelor's degree
law medicine	three college years
dentistry veterinary medicine	two college years

---

[1] S. Norma Feingold, *Scholarships, Fellowships, and Loans* (Boston: Bellman Publishing, 1949–1962). Four volumes.
[2] *Meeting Manpower Needs in Science and Technology Report Number One: Graduate Training in Engineering, Mathematics, and Physical Sciences.* A Report of the President's Science Advisory Committee, (Washington, D.C.: Government Printing Office, 1962), p. 9.

agriculture   high school diploma
architecture
business
engineering
forestry
home economics
nursing
optometry
pharmacy
teaching

There are numbers of variations to these standards. Most medical students (about three-fourths) and a substantial number of dental and law students have completed at least four years of college before entering professional school. Many universities permit students to enter professional schools only after two years of general college work, in effect establishing two years of college as a prerequisite for the fields listed above as requiring only high school graduation.

An educational requirement, although important, is hardly sufficient. Most professional schools apply other measures so they will not have to accept automatically all those who complete the minimum educational requirements. In this respect, they are more fortunate than some of their parent universities, particularly those that are state-supported. Some states compel public colleges and universities to accept all graduates of accredited high schools without further qualifications. As many as one-fourth of the freshmen entering these institutions depart from the campus at the end of the first semester, presumably satisfied with a system that gives them the opportunity to fail.

Luckily, this wasteful and painful system has not been applied to professional schools in the United States. Professional schools in the United States select students in advance of admission and many of them spend an inordinate amount of time in doing so. The duties of an admission committee member in a school of medicine, for example, are so demanding that faculty members quail at the thought of spending more than one term in its service.

The schools use many devices to determine which applicants will make the best students. All schools use past grade averages as one set of criteria. Students who have not done well in undergraduate work, although passing, cannot meet the demands of a professional school. Many schools have established a cutoff point for grade averages. If a student's record falls below that point, he is excluded. If it is above that point, he can compete with other applicants for admission.

Grade-point averages are only one indicator of intelligence and of accomplishment. As the number of applicants increases, more refined measures are needed. The grading systems of different colleges and high schools are not uniform. Some colleges grade at least one letter higher than others, and the work of some is not thorough regardless of grades. To offset these deficiencies, a good many professional schools require applicants to take achievement and aptitude tests. These not only supplement the grade-point averages, they sometimes measure other attributes as well.

For schools in some professions, admission tests are given nationally and are offered periodically at various centers around the country. They are scored at the national headquarters, and the results are sent to schools which the student has named. These professions include medicine, which administers the Medical College Aptitude Test through the Association of American Medical Colleges, and nursing, which also administers a test through the National League for Nursing. Law uses the Educational Testing Service (ETS) to administer the Law School Admission Test; nineteen schools of business use the ETS to administer the Admission Test for Graduate Study in Business. Some professions, such as education and clinical psychology, which give their advanced work through the graduate school, use more general tests. They may use the Graduate Record Examination, also administered by the ETS, or the Miller Analogies Test, administered by the Psychological Corporation of New York.

Does this complex of prerequisites, grade averages, and tests provide an effective means of selecting the competent and rejecting the inadequate student, or does the complex even increase the likelihood of choosing wisely? Neither question can be answered with finality, although the value of the procedures has been the subject of study for some time.

It is difficult to test the validity of admission procedures because the possible performance of students who are rejected cannot be compared with that of students who are admitted. But such evidence as has been accumulated shows that tests when used with grade averages do improve the selection of students. The ETS found that scores on the Admisison Test for Graduate Study in Business were somewhat better than undergraduate grade averages for predicting average grades in the first year of graduate study, but it also discovered that the best prediction is obtained by using a combination of undergraduate grade averages and test scores. In studies of the effects of using the Graduate Record Examination and the Miller Analogies Test, similar conclusions have been reached.

Performance in previous schools and tests of intelligence and aptitude help to exclude the unfit. To reach conclusions on the even more intangible traits which are significant for professional students, admission committees use additional devices—letters of recommendation, interviews, written autobiographies, and so on. Each of these has its place, and each can be used to aid in choice. But no device can guarantee accuracy. There are too many immeasurables—of motivation, of emotional tangles, of "late-blooming," of economic pressures.

Because of this fact, admission procedures can never be expected to provide perfect answers to the question of who should be admitted. By selection of students, professional schools have increased the quality and effectiveness of the professions. The use of admission procedures to guide selection is justified by the results. But professional educators must not push their luck too far. A test, a grade average, an interview, gives an approximation and only that. Schools should not place total dependence on their admissions procedures. The door to admission might well be held open to a few students who do not meet the requirements of the admission procedure. By so doing the school can compare the performance of those selected by approved procedures and those selected by less refined methods. Professional educators might well ponder the results of the so-called "Eight-Year Study" directed by the Progressive Education Association in the thirties. In it, selected universities found that students admitted from the experimental schools without regard to set requirements but merely upon recommendation of their high school principals were significantly more successful than their more conventionally admitted fellow students.[3]

The results of selection. Professions attract different kinds of students. And, because they vary in the demands they place upon

---

[3] Dean Chamberlin, *et al., Did They Succeed in College?* (New York: Harper & Row, Publishers, 1942).

their members, they select different kinds of students. Distinct variations can be noted, therefore, between the kinds of students that enter the field of chemistry and the kind that enter business, for example.

Differences in intelligence have been studied and assessed more fully than have other characteristics. The most famous study was based on the draft deferment tests conducted by the Educational Testing Service in the summer of 1951. The Service tested nearly 340,000 men students. It analyzed a random sample of 10 per cent to see whether it could identify distinctions among student groups. It discovered that engineering, physical science, and mathematics students stood highest on its tests, with biological science, social science, humanities, and business and commerce students a second somewhat lower group. Agriculture and education students fell into the bottom group. The students, it must be remembered, were all undergraduate men, and the results in education may have been distorted by the fact that many students, particularly those who intended to enter secondary teaching, were probably classified by their subject field rather than by "education." Nevertheless, even with these cautions, the conclusion that there are major differences among professions in the average intelligence of their students is inescapable.[4]

The distinctions made by the Selective Service tests can be supported by other data. Wolfle, in his detailed study of manpower in the United States, concluded that "some fields attract, or admit, students of a higher intelligence level than are attracted to other fields. . . ."[5] His further computations show that among undergraduate fields intelligence scores rank in the declining order of engineering, nursing, business and commerce, and education. In fields requiring some undergraduate prerequisites, the declining order is psychology, medicine, law, and social work.

Two more comments need to be made. The ranks given above should not be interpreted to mean that all students in one field are superior in intelligence test results to all students in other fields. There is much overlapping. Furthermore, other characteristics be-

[4] Educational Testing Service, *A Summary of Statistics on Selective Service Qualifying Test* (Princeton, N.J.: Educational Testing Service, 1952), p. 16.

[5] Dael Wolfle, *America's Resources of Specialized Talent* (New York: Harper & Row, Publishers, 1954), p. 197.

sides intelligence are important to practice of the professions. These attributes have been less subject to testing than intelligence and the results have not been accepted as easily. Some work has been done, however. Morris Rosenberg discovered that engineers had low scores in "faith in people," as measured by his indices, even though their intelligence was of the highest.[6] Many engineers would probably make poor elementary school teachers, and vice versa.

Evaluation of Performance

Having selected and admitted students, the professional school must find ways of evaluating their performance so that it can judge whether or not they have met the minimum requirements which the school establishes for its graduates. No school has fully solved the problem, since no method of evaluation is wholly satisfactory. Educators in the professions have come to recognize, however, that there are many ways to evaluate student performance, and that the pen-and-paper essay form of answering questions posed by the instructor may not be the most useful form in all situations.

Some fields use national tests which are scored by persons other than the students' instructors, but this method is in the minority. The Yale University School of Medicine uses the national board examinations at the end of the second and the fourth years rather than its own examinations to judge the success of its students. Some other medical schools require that their students take these examinations, but use a number of other examinations and tests to measure student performance.

Furthermore, the school in each profession which is subject to licensing by the state must prepare its students to meet the requirements of the state boards of licensure, or run the risk of producing graduates who will be unable to enter practice. Most examining boards are composed of members of the profession. Their examinations usually combine tests on the knowledge underlying the profession and upon skills of practice. In dentistry, for example, the test will often include a part where the new graduate will perform some of the tasks of the profession, and will be judged by his success in doing so.

---

[6] Morris Rosenberg, *Occupations and Values* (Glencoe, Ill.: The Free Press, 1967), Table 9, p. 27.

Testing for knowledge is quite different from testing for skills of application. A professional school usually makes an attempt to do both. It will set up simulated situations for which the student must find and execute desirable solutions. A social worker may be asked to conduct an interview with a potential client, for example, under the eye of an instructor who will decide whether his skills are sufficient to allow him to begin practice. A resident in psychiatry may conduct a therapy session with a patient behind a one-way screen while the instructor watches and listens.

A student's skills in application will be assessed during the field experience or internship when the student is in daily contact with the problems of the profession. Instructors sometimes use anecdotal records in which they describe the duties and responsibilities of the student and indicate how well he has performed his assignments. In teacher education, a number of schools require that the student maintain a log-book, a sort of professional diary, of the events of the field experience. The instructor reviews the log-books to find clues to the speed with which students are developing understanding and skill. A graduate architect during his period as "architect-in-training" keeps a log-book which he sends periodically to the American Institute of Architects for review.

Few instructors use all the devices that are available for evaluating a student's progress. George E. Miller, and others,[7] in suggesting ways by which instructors in medical schools can improve their evaluation of students' performance, describe and evaluate 12 methods. These include: for assessing knowledge—the essay examination, the oral examination, and the objective examination (in its various forms of true-false, multiple-choice, completion, and matching); for assessing performance—observational techniques, including the anecdotal record, the check list, and the rating scale; and for measuring attitudes, a more difficult task—the interview and the log-diary. For the sake of completeness, Dr. Miller and his colleagues also discuss the questionnaire, peer ratings, the filmed interview, and problem solving. Finally, they discuss grades and grading, pointing out that grades are designed for a number of purposes, including such disparate ends as serving as evidence for promotion or retention and as a means of motivating students to

---

[7] George E. Miller, *et al., Teaching and Learning in Medical School* (Cambridge, Mass., Harvard University Press, 1961), p. 283.

expend greater effort on their studies. The studies reinforce one conclusion which many instructors have reached. "The unfortunate history of academic grades as a reward for learning has made symbol chasers of most students, including medical students."[8] The authors believe that the field of student evaluation is so important that they devote six of seventeen chapters to it. Except for the field of teacher education, other professions have not devoted this amount of attention to the problem. It should be an area of greater concern.

Counseling

For years colleges and professional schools have maintained health services for students, since they recognize that the demands upon a student may affect his health, and certainly his state of health will affect his performance. Recognition that students have needs for other sorts of aid, such as counseling on emotional and academic problems, has been more grudging. The professional school of the early part of the century sometimes prided itself on its policy of sink-or-swim, maintaining that the school's responsibility ended when it gave students the opportunity to learn through library, lecture, and laboratory. If they ran into emotional difficulties while doing so, the fact merely demonstrated their unworthiness to become practitioners.

This haughty attitude is diminishing, although some recalcitrant professors still refer to student counselors as "boy scoutmasters." Many professional schools have assistant deans for students who develop and coordinate programs of admissions, promotions, and counseling. These assistant deans are the first point of contact for students. They often arrange for members of the faculty to do most of the counseling, except for severely disturbed students who need assistance of persons with greater training.

Schools which have established counseling activities have retained a number of students, many of them with great potential ability, who might otherwise have been lost to the school and the profession. Their success is great enough to suggest that all professional schools should carefully consider whether or not the needs of their students for counseling are being met.

---

8 *Ibid.*

Principles to Follow

1. Regardless of field, each student a professional school selects should be judged to have:
   a. An active, inquiring intelligence of high order;
   b. A stable personality;
   c. A commitment to the field;
   d. Sufficient self-confidence to permit flexibility and experimentation.

2. In addition, schools for each profession should join with members of the profession in determining the qualities required and the emphasis which each quality should receive. A profession should not merely accept what another profession has decided.

3. The profession and its schools should join efforts in recruiting sufficient numbers of qualified students through whatever means are effective.

4. Schools should select students, in so far as possible, in accordance with the characteristics which they and the profession have defined as desirable for the profession.

5. Schools should encourage instructors to experiment with a variety of ways to evaluate the performance of students, including evaluations of performance in class work and field instruction. If possible, some national evaluation of students should be made to provide comparisons with the quality of graduates produced at other schools.

6. Professional schools should provide means by which students may obtain health and counseling services when needed, and persons of special competence should be available when needed.

7. The quality of students will limit or enhance the quality of graduates. The profession and the schools should maintain as high a quality of student body as it possibly can while satisfying the numerical needs for persons to enter the profession. If a choice is necessary, it will be preferable to organize the profession so that subsidiary personnel take much of the routine responsibilities from the professional practitioners.

CHAPTER VII

Problems of the Future

Education for the professions has come a long, long way since it depended upon the teaching of practitioners who were often as interested in money and status as they were in the instruction of youth. Since 1900, the proprietary school has virtually disappeared. In its place, the professional school has emerged, first as a separate entity largely directed by the immediate interests of the profession, and later as an integral part of universities. These advances, for they are major advances, rest upon a number of forces—increase in knowledge, growth of an educational system, greater sophistication of the consumer of professional services, and a rapidly rising standard of living. Each of these forces added its impetus to change, and has now made the isolated professional school an anomaly, even when operated by the university itself. The Medical School of Stanford University, for example, moved from San Francisco to Palo Alto at the cost of a brand-new plant, in order to become more a part of the University. The University of Florida and West Virginia University chose to locate their new health schools in the small towns of the universities rather than in the larger cities of their states.

Other fields show similar tendencies. Engineering schools, once set apart from universities as too vocational, are now established divisions of many institutions. Teachers' colleges, which arose from the two-year normal schools, have expanded into arts and sciences colleges, and some are on the way to becoming universities. Separated schools of law are still scattered throughout the country, but almost all law schools with national reputations are parts of universities.

Nursing is an exception. Most nurses graduate from hospital schools, not from universities. The National League for Nursing recognizes the limitations of this sort of training, and is working steadily to supplement it with the collegiate training of nursing schools in universities. Even here, therefore, the trend is toward the university rather than toward the separated professional school.

The university has greatly aided the professional school, but the future still holds problems. Some of these are discussed in the following pages.

The Problem of Growing Demands
for Professional Service

As the professional school has moved into the university, it has placed upon the university the responsibility of educating sufficient numbers of professional persons to accomplish the tasks which the profession has undertaken. Demands for professionally trained people continue to grow, and the end is not yet in sight. Because the population of the United States is increasing continuously, medicine is contemplating twenty-two new medical schools merely to maintain the present ratio of physicians to population. Dentistry would also like to increase its ratio.

The estimate for 1970 of 7,000,000 college students will require many more college teachers, and the rapid expansion of elementary and secondary schools will also demand their share of teachers. In social work the problem is extremely severe. Its publication, *Social Work Education,* points out that "upwards of 15,000 persons would have to be recruited annually to replace those leaving the field, to staff necessary expansion of existing services, and to man newly developing services. This estimate does not take account of the full expansion of services that would be required by the recent rapid growth in population."[1] Or it might be added, the expected future growth of population. Against this minimum need for 15,000 graduates annually to meet the needs of the profession even on its present basis, the graduate schools of social work in the United States and Canada graduated 2476 students with master's degrees in June, 1962.[2] The chances of meeting the needs for social workers with graduates of master's degree programs appear to be so remote as to be nonexistent. And yet the universities and the schools of social work which they harbor continue to maintain that

---

[1] "Fact Sheet on Social Work Manpower and Social Work Education, 1962–1963." *Social Work Education,* published by the Council on Social Work Education, Vol. XI, No. 1. (February, 1963), 28.
[2] *Ibid.*

most of the needs of the profession can be met with master's degree programs.

Many solutions will be attempted. The larger proportion of college-age youth who will attend college will provide a bigger reservoir from which professional students may be drawn, but it is hardly likely that present and impending shortages can be satisfied merely by the involuntary effect of increased college populations. No, this will not be enough. The universities and the professions both have their work cut out for them, if they are to meet the demands of society for professional persons.

Universities must help the professions to recognize the difficulties which the universities face in meeting the needs of the professions. The universities cannot satisfy the demand without aid from the professions, both in securing greater supporting income for the universities and in organizing themselves more effectively for discharging their responsibilities. Professions can no longer afford the luxury of using their members at anything lower than their top skills. Professional people must not be expected to do routine tasks which can be delegated to persons with less training and less capacity. Doctors have made these delegations to nurses and hospital administrators; dentists have made these delegations to dental hygienists and dental assistants; engineers have made those delegations to engineering technicians, and so on. Such delegations have been and are being made. They must be increased, if the professions expect the schools to satisfy their needs.

Members of a profession who have executed all the tasks, even the most routine, are fearful of accepting the help of ancillary personnel. Their hesitations must be overcome by vigorous leadership from their national organizations and their schools. They must recognize that continuing shortages of fully trained professional persons cause dangers which the professions can ill afford. Unless the shortages are met, the public will turn to unqualified people to perform the services. Without physicians, the public will turn to neighbors, friends, and faith-healers for medical advice and guidance. Without teachers, a community will turn to glorified baby sitters to keep the schools open. Without social workers a city may employ untrained party faithfuls.

Recruitment is important, for students should know the possibilities in the professions. Scholarships and fellowships, as well as loan funds, can attract additional students, but even with the greatest amount of effort, recruitment alone cannot close the chasm which yawns between the number of social workers, for example, graduated annually and the defined need for persons in this profession. The problem of numbers can be met only by using every possible strategy, including recruitment, reorganization of the profession, and special training plans for persons already in the profession. When the universities embraced the professional schools and urged the professions to admit only those persons who had completed the prescribed college course, they also assumed responsibility for producing enough graduates to staff the profession. Their task is not complete if they concern themselves only with graduating students whose education is of high quality. This they must do, but they must do more. The schools must graduate enough students to meet the needs of the professions. Anything less than this is dangerous for the professions and the schools.

The Problem of Group or Organized Practice

The number of professional people has increased substantially over the past years, but the number is still insufficient to meet the needs and demands of the public. Furthermore, the explosion of knowledge has made it impossible for any practitioner to command the full knowledge available to him. As one result, more and more often the idea of solitary practice—the doctor in the one-hoss shay —has dissolved into the actuality of the clinic where specialists combine their talents into a group practice which more nearly meets the needs of the public than any single physician.[3]

This agglomeration of specialists has occurred in the medical, legal, and architectural professions. It has affected dentistry less. But in most of the other professions—engineering, teaching, nursing, social work, forestry, and to a growing extent in agriculture— the professional person is no longer, if he ever was, the self-

---

[3] For a social scientist's view of medicine, see Anne Ramsay Somers "Conflict, Accommodation, and Progress: Some Socio-Economic Observations on Medical Education and the Practicing Profession," *The Journal of Medical Education,* Vol. 38, No. 6 (June, 1963), 466–478. She says, "It is the solo GP, that beloved but increasingly anachronistic figure of fact and fancy, who remains the semimystical ideal of large parts of the profession and the public alike, and thus constitutes a major barrier to the more rational organization of *both* medical care and medical organization."

employed, self-directing practitioner in the image which the words "professional person" bring to mind. Instead, these professions typically are practiced in institutions, under professional leadership of administrators and supervisors and lay leadership of boards of trustees. In fact, the future of the professions is moving toward the "institutional" practitioner rather than the "private" practitioner.

This shift inevitably creates problems for the professional person. Within a hierarchy, he is no longer held solely responsible for his acts and their consequences, but must share responsibility with other persons. As the size of group practice increases, the dangers of diffuse responsibility and of committee paralysis grow. The approval of superiors and colleagues may become more important than decisive action. When the professional man exchanges the fee system for the security of a salary, he may try to follow the safe rather than the experimental course.

How can the professions, faced with these difficulties, maintain their independence of action so that their special and crucial skills will not be lost in a fog of organized, institutional procedures? How can they maintain their integrity of decision, based upon their judgment of what is best for the client, and stand ready to be judged upon the consequences of that action? In other words, how can professional men maintain their individual responsibility within the context of group action?

These are difficult questions. They cannot be answered quickly or easily. The professions will undoubtedly hammer out answers that satisfy them as they face the need for functioning effectively within groups. Engineering, social work, nursing, and teaching have functioned within groups for much of their existence. Normally, their work is done within the hierarchy of the industrial plant or engineering firm, the hospital, the school, or the social work agency. They have learned either to accommodate themselves to the restrictions of existence in an organization, or they have established policies by which their professional freedom is maintained in spite of occasional encroachments.

In fact, it is possible, unlikely as it may seem, for the professional person within an organization to be able to enjoy a freedom which the private practioner may lack. The practitioner is dependent upon the favor of his clients who are willing to pay him a fee, and their judgment may be swayed by wholly extraneous reasons, ones other than the professional competence of the practitioner. They may not like his religion, or his politics, or his wife, and they can easily destroy his practice through withholding their patronage. But look, instead, at the protection of professional responsibility which the concept of academic freedom supplies to the university faculty member. He is protected by a doctrine that upholds his right to teach and publish whatever his research discovers, regardless of its unpopularity with presidents, boards of trustees, or potential donors. His income is theoretically inviolate, so long as he discharges his professional responsibilities. He is protected by a concept which maintains that he cannot function effectively except when he is free to follow his professional convictions. If he tempers these to the winds of lay opinion, his usefulness is diminished by the exact amount of his deviation from what he conceives to be truth. His significance lies precisely in his ability to ignore the consequences of his professional conclusions. Only in this way, society has discovered, can his full contribution be obtained.[4]

A similar doctrine of what might be called "professional freedom" must be developed for those professional persons who work more and more in congeries rather than alone. They must be protected in their right to act within their responsible roles as professional people through a doctrine comparable to tenure on the campus. As one wise research man once said, "Supervision does not keep a research man on his toes; it keeps him on his knees." And kneeling is not an effective position for a professional man. He must be permitted, encouraged, and supported to stand on the basis of his professional conclusions, regardless of the hierarchy in which he functions. He must be so imbued with the significance of his contributions that he is willing to resign from positions in which he cannot exercise professional freedom and responsibility. He must help to establish an ethic for the organization in which he works, just as the professor, banding with colleagues in the American Association of University Professors, has been able to establish an ethic on the campus which the universities and colleges accept and attempt to follow, even when the course to be taken differs greatly from what a board of trustees would adopt for governing a business organization.

---

[4] See Walter P. Metzger, *Academic Freedom in the Age of the University* (New York: Columbia University Press, 1961). Columbia Paperback Edition.

An ethic for an organization will be possible only if the individual professional person conducts himself within the limits of the ethical code of his profession. If he does that, he is in a strong position to press for the organization to recognize and follow the ethic of professional freedom. He can be even more effective in achieving this end if he will join with colleagues in other professions to indicate clearly the needs of the professional person. His responsibilities, his obligations, and his freedoms must be described with clarity. And the directors of organizations that violate the principles of professional freedom should be brought to task by appropriate reports and censure which would be disseminated sufficiently for other professional persons to guide their actions in light of the organization's deficiencies. Group practice, in partnerships and in hierarchies, is certain to increase. Professional people should help leaders of these organizations to understand the conditions that will encourage professional work of high quality.

What does this future of group practice mean to professional education? It means, first of all, that the professional student must recognize that group practice is a response to conditions which place a premium on specialization. An understanding of the history of the profession in its various manifestations would be helpful. It also means that professional education should help students to understand the conditions which must be met before the professional person is willing to enter a group. He has an obligation to his professional status to make sure that he does not enter situations in which effective practice cannot be attained. It must also help the professional student to recognize that he must follow the ethic of the profession as meticulously in an organization as he would if practicing alone. Finally, professional education must instill attitudes of respect for all manifestations of the profession which worthily discharge their professional functions. It is too simple a distinction to maintain that all private practice is somehow imbued with good and all group practice shot through with incompetence. Experience in all types of practice would be helpful in dispelling notions that only certain forms of practice have validity.

The Problem of Social Responsibility

The monopoly which a profession enjoys is necessary for its practice (see Chapter I). Monopoly places upon the profession a profound obligation to function in such a way that society will benefit as greatly as possible. Unless this ethic is maintained, the profession may use its special knowledge for self-benefit and for exploitation of clients. If it does, it becomes a danger rather than a benefit to society, and its privileged status will be removed in order to protect the people it once served.

This much is almost self-evident. But the responsibility of the profession goes much further than merely to shun exploitation. It has an obligation to supply its services in as full measure as possible for as low a social cost as it can manage. In other words, the profession has an obligation to increase the social efficiency of its services, and to take the leadership in doing so.

This kind of leadership is difficult. It requires a flexible, dedicated group of professional persons, who are unwilling to become tied to any one method of providing the services they control, and who are constantly looking for ways to improve their services. They therefore are constantly searching for:

1. *New knowledge that will increase the effectiveness of the services.*
The social responsibility of the profession requires that it support and encourage the search for new knowledge and more desirable methods of practice. A profession which does not encourage research and experimentation is not discharging its social obligations. When the American Nurses Association increased its dues for the specific purpose of aiding research projects on nursing, it was discharging its obligation to search for new knowledge. The field of clinical psychology has accepted this obligation so firmly that it refuses to consider seriously the possibility of professional schools of clinical psychology, preferring rather to have the clinical psychologist educated in the atmosphere of experimental psychology to emphasize the value that it places on research. The examples could be multiplied many times.

2. *New methods by which problems can be prevented or reduced.*
The physician and the lawyer are thought of as persons who aid individuals to regain their health or obtain justice. Such individual service will always have its place, even though it probably grew out of the situation where the noble retained the services of the professional man for his own use. But the individual service concept, the cure of the disease or the winning of the law suit, cannot by itself maintain health or justice. More fundamental approaches are needed. When the physician becomes a public health officer, he may prevent hundreds of cases of typhoid fever by maintaining a pure water supply, and the lawyer elected to the legislature may bring justice to hundreds of disadvantaged persons by

welfare legislation. A profession which limits its services to treatment of individual manifestations cannot hope to be fully effective. Education never became effective for any except the few when it depended upon tutoring in private homes. Teachers must support other methods of education than those received in schools if they want their communities to be composed of educated persons. Teachers have typically, therefore, worked for public libraries, supported book stores, praised educational TV programs, and guided adult education activities. A profession must also push for prevention of problems, and it must find methods by which groups can receive as much knowledge of the profession as they can effectively use without dependence on the profession itself. A lay person can hardly fill his own teeth, but he can certainly learn to brush them.

3. *Methods of extending the services according to need.*

Ultimately, a profession's sense of social responsibility must stimulate it to the point where it tries to make sure that the service it can provide is available to all those that need it. A profession is unwilling to consider its services only as a luxury with which members of society can dispense at their pleasure. Instead, a profession, by definition, deals with matters of great human moment far beyond a reasonable definition of a luxury. Education, medical care, justice, effective work space, food and clothing, and many other kinds of services which the professions supply should be extended insofar as possible on a basis of need rather than ability to pay. The professions have always known this. The physician has expected to teach and to treat charity patients, the lawyer to be assigned by the court to defend the indigent when necessary, the community to care for the orphaned and the aged, and so on. The professions have gladly assumed these responsibilities. Sometimes, however, they have objected strenuously when the extension of the services for which they are responsible came about through insurance or public taxation. The vigorous discussion of medical care for the aged through social security programs is but one more item in the long history of extending essential services.

Education for the professions must aid its students in recognizing their responsibility to find ways of fulfilling unmet needs, even if this requires different methods of providing services. It is not enough for a teacher to do effective work in the classroom if there are large numbers of children whom the schools cannot reach. A social worker has responsibilities beyond the clients she can meet day by day. The engineer discharges part of his responsibility when he designs effective machines himself, but he has also an obligation to help see to it that the benefits of technology are given to others. Here again the professional school is faced with the problem of developing attitudes which make the profession fully effective as an instrument of social progress. It can do this with its curriculum, but it should also expose its students to situations where professional services have been lacking, and ask them to propose useful means by which those services can be brought to the situations.

The obligation should be made clear, but means of meeting it should also be sought, just as the appropriate remedy for an intestinal infection is suggested by a medical student undergoing a clinical clerkship.

As the professional school searches for and helps its students search for new knowledge in the field, for new methods of preventing or reducing the problems with which the professions deal, and for ways of extending the services of the profession to places where they are lacking, it is helping students to become instruments of social progress as well as practitioners of professions. A profession must lead as well as serve.[5]

The Problem of Educating for Research and Teaching as Well as Practice

Professional schools grew largely out of the demands of the professions for trained persons. In their simplest form, they prepared new entrants for the professions and did little with education for research or education for teaching. More recently professional schools have consciously accepted the obligation to educate students for careers in research and for careers in teaching, as well as for practice.

Some professions have lengthened the curriculum to prepare students who wish to teach or to undertake research careers. In medicine, for example, a student by taking additional courses may obtain a master's degree in addition to his doctor of medicine degree in order to qualify for a teaching and research position. If he is interested wholly in the medical sciences rather than in practice, he may take the doctor of philosophy degree in one of the medical sciences instead of the doctor of medicine degree. His career will usually be spent in teaching and research in a medical school, but he will not be qualified for medical practice. Nursing has defined the master's degree as desirable for teaching positions, even though it expects teachers to have been licensed as registered nurses also.

---

[5] Dr. Philip E. Blackerby, of the Kellogg Foundation, has proposed that dental schools establish departments of "social dentistry" to have "Primary responsibility for . . . those areas of dental education which contribute most directly to the social maturation and evolving professional philosophy of the student." "Rationale for a Department of Social Dentistry," *Journal of Dental Education*, Vol. 27, No. 2 (June, 1963), p. 121.

In engineering, nearly a third of new faculty members hold the doctor of philosophy degree.

These efforts to educate persons for teaching and research in the professions create a difficult situation. The practitioner has been the public symbol of the profession. He is beginning to share his status with the research man and the teacher. Nevertheless, the teacher or the research man is usually required to spend longer periods in preparation than the practitioner, although the practitioner enjoys greater status and income. Some professional schools are reducing the length of study by allowing students to acquire two degrees in combination within a much shorter time than the two could be acquired separately. Northwestern University has been doing this for some years with a combined program leading to the doctor of medicine and doctor of philosophy degrees. The University of Louisville began a similar program in 1963, under which a student can use the summer sessions for work toward the master of science degree, while pursuing his doctor of medicine degree during the regular sessions. Another two years at the end of the doctor of medicine program will make it possible for the student to obtain a doctor of philosophy degree also. The program will be restricted to a small number of exceptional students, but these are the very ones who are desperately needed in classrooms and teaching laboratories.

In spite of his longer period of education, the student who wishes to teach will lack experience in practice, unless he enters practice for a period before he begins his teaching. The clinical faculty member in a school of medicine does not suffer from this lack since he often has the responsibility of practicing in the teaching hospital. But other fields less frequently operate agencies which supply professional services. Faculty members can supplement their education by taking consultant positions, and can sometimes find summer work which adds to their experience in the profession. It is likely, however, that the desire of the teacher to practice also will diminish. He will discover that he can analyze a profession's needs without experiencing them in detail.

Ultimately, the problem is to make certain that the schools prepare enough teachers and researchers as well as practitioners. Professions must expand in numbers and in knowledge. They can do neither well without sufficient numbers of teachers and researchers.

Each profession must find ways of honoring research and teaching so that their prestige keeps pace with the prestige of practice.

When professions developed their distinctive bodies of knowledge and skills, they could no longer depend upon the lawyer's office or the hospital's lounge rooms for the education of the students. They had to obtain career teachers and career researchers. The Markle Foundation, the American Heart Association, and a number of government programs have established awards of "Career Investigators" under which a man of competence is supported for a number of years while he conducts research of interest to him. Dr. Willard C. Rappleye, President of the Josiah Macy, Jr. Foundation, has suggested that these awards be extended into "Career Professorships" in order to encourage qualified physicians to enter and remain in teaching.[7]

No profession has found a systematic, effective way of making sure that it obtains the teachers and research men it needs. In medicine, the training grants of the Public Health Service have encouraged students to enter studies leading to careers in research. But not enough is being done there or elsewhere to make sure that the number of teachers needed will be in the classroom when the students arrive. In fact, the surveys of teacher supply are all depressing reading. Universities and their professional schools will obtain fewer rather than more fully qualified persons for their faculties. One problem of the future is to find ways of changing this situation sufficiently to satisfy the needs of the schools.

The Problem of Financing Professional Education

Precise figures are missing, but every college administrator recognizes that the programs of professional schools are among the most expensive on the campus. Their cost is increasing steadily as the standards of the professions rise.

There are many reasons for the expense. When professional education depended largely upon lectures by practitioners, the students could pay most of the cost. But once professional educators agreed that the scientific background of a professional field was essential to practice, costs began to rise. The sciences could not be effectively

---

[7] Willard C. Rappleye, *The Current Era of Medical Education: Excerpts from President's Review* (New York: Josiah Macy, Jr. Foundation, 1961–62), p. 24.

taught in large lecture halls. They depended on laboratory exercises performed by the students as a means of retracing the steps which led to major discoveries and of learning the procedures of the scientific method. Furthermore, the practice of some of the professional schools, notably in medicine, dentistry, and teaching, to establish and operate agencies of the profession in the teaching hospital, the dental clinic, and the demonstration school added substantial costs. In off-campus agencies, supervision of internships is time-consuming and expensive, for the ratio of students to instructors must be very low. The competition between universities and practice tended to elevate salaries of professional faculty members to points comparable with the income of practitioners, which usually exceeded those of college teachers by considerable margins. Finally, the addition of research, for advancement of knowledge, to the aims of professional education increased costs. Research in the physical sciences requires extremely expensive equipment to deal with the almost infinitely large and infinitesimally small objects which the sciences now consider. The problem of merely maintaining subscriptions to scientific journals in sufficient numbers can overwhelm what once was an adequate library budget.

To offset these rising costs, the professional schools have searched diligently for new sources of funds. They have raised notable amounts themselves, first from philanthropic foundations and voluntary health agencies, and more recently from the various federal agencies. So successful have the schools been that they are often able to finance a major portion of their expenses through funds other than those obtained from student tuition, endowments, or regular appropriations. One large university receives nearly two-thirds of its total budget from the federal government. In effect, it has become almost a national university in financial support as well as in clientele.

Given all this, the stresses caused by these forms of support are clearly visible. Because needs of the government agencies are more closely related to the natural sciences than to the social sciences and humanities, these parts of the universities are less able to obtain funds. They suffer in comparison. They are asking that the federal government establish a National Humanities Foundation to support the humanities with as much vigor as it now supports the natural sciences. They are implying that they, too, can serve as instruments of national policy.

The professional schools from the beginning of their existence have been considered as instruments devoted to achieving predetermined ends, first of trained people to enter and continue the professions and then of research to expand the knowledge on which the functions of the profession rest. It is little wonder that the professional schools have accepted the role of instrument easily. They had established it long ere the federal government wanted them to act in that direction.

The future of professional education seems to be based upon federal funds, not just for research projects but for general support. Costs have risen so high in many professional fields that they cannot be met except by funds drawn from the widest possible base. That base is the federal government. The 1963 Congress expanded federal support into the instructional phases of the health professions, and broadened support for other professional schools and the natural sciences. Tax support is essential for professional schools to fulfill their objectives. The only source of tax funds available to private universities in most states is the federal government. As a result, the greatest push for federal funds has come from the private universities, which a few years ago were hesitant to accept support from any public body. With the collapse of their opposition, the policy questions relating to tax support of higher education have been largely resolved. Only the questions of amount and extent remain. Professional schools in many fields, because of need and because of contribution, will receive substantial support from federal funds within the next twenty-five years.

Bibliography

GENERAL

Anderson, G. Lester, *et al.*, *Education for the Professions*. The Sixty-First Yearbook of the National Society for The Study of Education. Chicago: University of Chicago Press, 1962.

Blauch, Lloyd, ed., *Accreditation in Higher Education*. Washington, D.C.: Government Printing Office, 1959.

——, *Education for the Professions*. Washington, D.C.: Government Printing Office, 1955.

Carr-Saunders, A. M. and P. A. Wilson, *The Professions*. Oxford: Clarendon Press, 1933.

Landis, Benson Y., ed., "Ethical Standards and Professional Conduct," *The Annals of the American Academy of Political and Social Science*, Vol. 297 (January, 1955).

Lynn, Kenneth S., ed., "The Professions" *Daedulus*, Vol. 94, No. 2 (Fall, 1963).

McGlothlin, William J., *Patterns of Professional Education*. New York: G. P. Putnam's Sons, 1960.

McGrath, Earl J., *Liberal Education in the Professions*. New York: Bureau of Publications, Columbia University, Teachers College, 1959.

Rosenberg, Morris, *Occupations and Values*. Glencoe, Ill.: The Free Press, 1957.

Selden, William K., *Accreditation: A Struggle Over Standards in Higher Education*. New York: Harper & Row, Publishers, 1960.

Smith, Elliott Dunlap, ed., *Education for Professional Responsibility*. Pittsburgh: Carnegie Press, 1948.

Teacher Supply and Demand in Universities, Colleges, and Junior Colleges, 1961–62 and 1962–63. Washington, D.C.: National Education Association, 1963.

Wolfle, Dael, *America's Resources of Specialized Talent*. New York: Harper & Row, Publishers, 1954.

ARCHITECTURE

Bannister, Turpin C., ed., *The Architect at Mid-Century: Evolution and Achievement*. New York: Reinhold Publishing Corporation, 1954.

BUSINESS

Gordon, Robert A. and James E. Howell, *Higher Education for Business*. New York: Columbia University Press, 1959.

Pierson, Frank C., *et al., The Education of American Businessmen*. New York: McGraw-Hill Book Co., 1959.

DENTISTRY

Hollinshead, Byron S., Director, *The Survey of Dentistry*. Washington, D.C.: American Council on Education, 1961.

ENGINEERING

Grinter, Linton E., *Chm., Report on Evaluation of Engineering Education*. Urbana, Illinois: American Society for Engineering Education, 1955.

Gullette, George A., *ed., General Education in Engineering. A Report of the Humanistic-Social Research Project*. Urbana, Illinois: American Society for Engineering Education, 1956.

Wilson, James W. and Edward H. Lyons, *Work-Study College Programs*. New York: Harper & Row, Publishers, 1961.

FORESTRY

Dana, Samuel and Evert W. Johnson, *Forestry Education in America: Today and Tomorrow*. Washington, D.C.: Society of American Foresters, 1963.

HOME ECONOMICS

American Home Economics Association, *Home Economics in Higher Education*. Washington, D.C.: The Association, 1949.

LAW

Association of American Law Schools, *Anatomy of Modern Legal Education*. St. Paul, Minn.: West Publishing Co., 1961.

Harno, Albert J., *Legal Education in the United States*. San Francisco: Bancroft-Whitney Co., 1953.

MEDICINE

Deitrick, John E. and Robert C. Berson, *Medical Schools in the United States at Mid-Century*. New York: McGraw-Hill Book Co., 1953.

Flexner, Abraham, *Medical Education in the United States and Canada*. Boston: Updyke, Merrymount Press, 1910.

Miller, George E., *et al., Teaching and Learning in Medical School*. Cambridge, Mass.: Harvard University Press, 1961.

NURSING

Bridgman, Margaret, *Collegiate Education for Nursing*. New York: Russell Sage Foundation, 1953.

Brown, Esther Lucile, *Nursing for the Future*. New York: Russell Sage Foundation, 1948.

PHARMACY

Blauch, Lloyd E. and George L. Webster, *The Pharmaceutical Curriculum*. Washington, D.C.: American Council on Education, 1952.

PLANNING

Perloff, Harvey S., *Education for Planning: City, State, and Regional.* Baltimore: The Johns Hopkins University Press, 1957.

PSYCHOLOGY

Raimy, Victor C., *ed., Training in Clinical Psychology.* Englewood Cliffs, N. J.: Prentice-Hall, Inc., 1950.

Roe, Anne, *et al., Graduate Education in Psychology.* Washington, D.C.: American Psychological Association, 1959.

SOCIAL WORK

Boehm, Werner W., Director, *The Social Work Curriculum Study.* 13 Vols. New York: Council on Social Work Education, 1959.

Towle, Charlotte, *The Learner in Education for the Professions.* Chicago: University of Chicago Press, 1954.

TEACHING

Conant, James Bryant, *The Education of American Teachers.* New York: McGraw-Hill Book Co., 1963.

Lieberman, Myron, *Education as a Profession.* Englewood Cliffs, N. J.: Prentice-Hall, Inc., 1956.

THEOLOGY

Niebuhr, H. Richard, Daniel Day Williams, and James M. Gustafson, *The Advancement of Theological Education.* New York: Harper and Row, Publishers, 1957.

VETERINARY MEDICINE

Bierer, B. W., *A Short History of Veterinary Medicine in America.* East Lansing, Michigan: Michigan State University Press, 1955.

Index

University of Texas, medical school
planned, 20

V

Veterinary medicine (includes veterinary medical schools and veterinary medical education), 38,
39, 41, 73, 75, 76
curriculum:
length, 46
organization, 48
prerequisites, 86

W

West Virginia University, 95
Western Reserve University School of
Medicine, 50
Whitehead, Alfred North, 55
Wolfle, Dael, 90
Woodrow Wilson fellowships, 61

Y

Yale University, 91